OECD
ECONOMIC SURVEYS

SPAIN

ORGANISATION FOR ECONOMIC CO-OPERATION AND DEVELOPMENT

Pursuant to article 1 of the Convention signed in Paris on 14th December 1960, and which came into force on 30th September 1961, the Organisation for Economic Co-operation and Development (OECD) shall promote policies designed:

- to achieve the highest sustainable economic growth and employment and a rising standard of living in Member countries, while maintaining financial stability, and thus to contribute to the development of the world economy;
- to contribute to sound economic expansion in Member as well as non-member countries in the process of economic development; and
- to contribute to the expansion of world trade on a multilateral, non-discriminatory basis in accordance with international obligations.

The original Member countries of the OECD are Austria, Belgium, Canada, Denmark, France, the Federal Republic of Germany, Greece, Iceland, Ireland, Italy, Luxembourg, the Netherlands, Norway, Portugal, Spain, Sweden, Switzerland, Turkey, the United Kingdom and the United States. The following countries became Members subsequently through accession at the dates indicated hereafter: Japan (28th April 1964), Finland (28th January 1969), Australia (7th June 1971) and New Zealand (29th May 1973).

The Socialist Federal Republic of Yugoslavia takes part in some of the work of the OECD (agreement of 28th October 1961).

Publié également en français.

Table of contents

Tables

Diagrams

Text

This Survey is based on the Secretariat's study prepared for the annual review of Spain by the Economic and Development Review Committee on 11th April 1989.

After revisions in the light of discussions during the review, final approval of the Survey for publication was given by the Committee on 17th May 1989.

The previous Survey of Spain was issued in January 1988.

BASIC STATISTICS OF SPAIN

THE LAND

Area (1 000 sq. km)	504.8	Major cities, 1981 census,	
Agricultural area (1 000 sq. km) 1985	204.2	thousands inhabitants:	
		Madrid	3 188
		Barcelona	1 755
		Valencia	752
		Seville	654

THE PEOPLE

Population, 31-12-87, thousands	38 914	Civilian employment, 1988, thousands	11 773
Number of inhabitants per sq. km	77	By sector (percentage):	
Net natural increase (1986, thousands)	127	Agriculture	14.4
Migration (1986, thousands)	37	Industry	23.8
		Construction	8.7
		Services	53.1

PRODUCTION

Gross domestic product, 1987 (billion pesetas)	35 715	Gross domestic product at factor cost by origin,	
GDP per head, (1987 US $)	7 449	in 1987 (percentages):	
Gross fixed investment:		Agriculture	5
Per cent of GDP (1987)	20.7	Industry	30
Per head (US $) 1987	1 540	Construction	8
		Services	58

THE GENERAL GOVERNMENT

Public consumption, in 1987 (percentage of GDP)	14.4	Government revenue, in 1987 (percentage of GDP)	38
Fixed investment in 1987 (percentage of gross fixed capital formation)	16.8	General government deficit, in 1987 (percentage of GDP)	−3.6

FOREIGN TRADE

Exports of goods and services, 1987 (billion US $)	56.9	Imports of goods and services, 1987 (billion US $)	56.3
Exports of goods and services as a percentage of GDP, 1987	19.7	Imports of goods and services as a percentage of GDP, 1987	19.5
Exports 1987, percentage of merchandise exports, customs basis:		Imports 1987, percentage of merchandise imports, customs basis:	
Foodstuffs	17.6	Foodstuffs	10.1
Raw materials	3.7	Raw materials	8.4
Fuels and lubricants	6.2	Fuels and lubricants	16.4
Capital goods	14.7	Capital goods	23.8
Consumer goods	31.6	Consumer goods	19.8
Intermediate goods	26.2	Intermediate goods	21.6

THE CURRENCY

Monetary unit: Peseta		Currency units per US $, average of daily figures:	
		Year 1988	116.5
		April 1989	116.2

Note: An international comparison of certain basic statistics is given in an annex table.

Introduction

Since joining the European Communities in 1986 the Spanish economy has been in a phase of rapid expansion. In 1988, for the second year running, the growth of real GDP was around 5 per cent and the associated rise of employment of 3 per cent was the highest recorded in OECD Europe. With domestic demand continuing to grow faster than the economy's productive potential[1], imports have been boosted, shifting the current external balance into deficit to the tune of 1 per cent of GDP. Even so, the overall balance of payments again closed with a huge surplus, pushing the level of official reserves to a new record high of $40 billion. Despite heavy foreign exchange interventions, the peseta appreciated in effective terms, and even more so in real terms. This did not prevent inflation from reaccelerating in the second half of 1988, with the index of consumer prices rising by 5.8 per cent in the twelve months to December 1988.

In the face of rising inflationary pressure, monetary policy has been progressively tightened since September 1988. The Bank of Spain's intervention rate was raised in several steps to 13.8 per cent in April 1989, up from 10.5 per cent six months earlier, and the official target range for money supply growth in 1989 has been significantly reduced relative to the 1988 target. On the fiscal side, notwithstanding policy measures to support activity, strong "automatic stabiliser" effects resulted in a further decline of the general government deficit in 1988. For 1989, the prospects are for a continuation of the present broadly-based economic upswing, though decelerating business investment and increased pressure on productive resources will probably result in some slowdown of output growth. The inflation outlook is surrounded by greater uncertainty than usual: while increased trade union militancy for higher pay can be expected to push up unit labour costs, the tighter stance of monetary policy could limit the scope for price increases more effectively than hitherto, in particular if combined with further liberalisation measures in trade and services.

Part I of this Survey reviews the main factors behind the continued strength of the upturn and the reasons for the rebound of inflation. Part II, after discussing fiscal, monetary and supply-side policies, assesses the economic prospects for 1989 and 1990. Part III is devoted to issues arising from the size and growth of the public sector. International comparisons of public sector resource claims and provision of public services help to identify areas of relative weakness and strength, with respect both to the level and composition of expenditure and to the system of taxation and financing. Conclusions are presented in Part IV.

I. Economic developments in 1988

The Spanish economy has exhibited even greater dynamism over the past eighteen months or so than was projected in OECD, *Economic Survey of Spain*, January 1988. As can be inferred from comparisons of forecasts and outcomes shown in Table 1, this can partly be explained by the stronger underlying growth path in 1987, resulting in a bigger carry-over into 1988. The difference between initial projections and preliminary results is particularly striking in the case of gross fixed investment,

Table 1. **1987 and 1988 developments in retrospect**

Percentage change over previous year

	1985	1986	1987		1988	
	Outcome		Preliminary estimates[1]	Out-come	Projections[1]	Outcome Provisional
Private consumption	2.4	3.6	4½	5.5	3¼	4.5
Government consumption	4.6	5.7	6	8.7	4½	5.0
Gross fixed investment	4.1	10.0	14	14.6	8	14.0
Total domestic demand	2.9	6.1	16½	8.5	4½	6.9
Exports of goods and services	2.8	1.3	7½	5.9	4¼	6.3
Imports of goods and services	6.2	16.5	19	20.4	10	15.2
Foreign balance[2]	−0.5	−2.6	−2½	−2.8	−1½	−2.1
GDP at constant prices	2.3	3.3	4½	5.5	3½	5.0
Memorandum items :						
Total employment	−0.9	2.2	3½	3.1	2¼	2.9
Unemployment rate[3]	21.5	21.0	20¼	20.5	20¼	19.5
GDP price deflator	8.5	10.9	5½	5.9	4	5.7
Consumer price deflator	8.2	8.7	5½	5.4	4½	5.1
Current external balance						
(US$ billion)	(2.5)	(3.9)	(1½)	(0.0)	(−2)	(−3.6)
(Per cent of GDP)	(1.3)	(1.7)	(½)	(0.0)	(−½)	(−1.1)

1. See OECD *Economic Survey of Spain*, January 1988.
2. Contribution to growth of GDP.
3. Labour Force Survey data.
Source: OECD, *National Accounts* and OECD estimates.

11

which after a big rise of almost 15 per cent in 1987 experienced another jump of almost the same magnitude in 1988. This may be in large measure related to the under-prediction of continued massive foreign capital inflows and more generally the greater buoyancy of demand at home and abroad, permitting profits to rise even more strongly than was anticipated. In 1988, the increase in net foreign direct investment in business and real estate amounted to as much as 0.4 per cent of GDP and to nearly one-fourth of the increase in private investment[2]. With trends of all other major demand components steepening, the labour market situation improved more than projected and the general government net borrowing requirement diminished. On the other hand, the increased pressure of demand brought the process of disinflation to a halt and weakened the current balance-of-payments position more than had been projected.

Booming demand and output

As noted above, fixed investment continued to grow at about the same rapid rate as in 1987, thus constituting the principal source of demand growth. All components of investment participated in the boom though with uneven strength (Diagram 1). A pick-up of government investment broadly offset the "natural" slowdown of private investment from earlier unsustainably high rates. Within private investment the slowdown was mainly confined to investment in machinery and equipment, with its rate of increase (15 per cent in real terms) remaining however vigorous. The trend of private residential construction seems to have steepened, as suggested by the 66 per cent increase in new housing credits. Construction activity, stimulated by foreign companies' demand for offices, was particularly buoyant in Madrid and Barcelona where rents and real estate prices have been booming[3].

Business investment has not only been stimulated by high and growing profits and massive foreign capital injections, but has also been encouraged by increased pressure on resources and, most importantly, by favourable demand prospects at home and abroad. Thus, the volume of exports of manufactures expanded by as much as 9 per cent in 1988, almost twice as fast as in 1987. The growth of real disposable household income, remained at a high rate of some 5 per cent, mainly supported by steep rises in non-wage incomes and employment growth. This permitted private consumption to grow by 4½ per cent, only a little less than in the preceding couple of years. The increase in government consumption slowed down markedly though, at around 5 per cent, still exceeding what may be considered a sustainable medium-to-longer-term trend rate.

Diagram 1. **SELECTIVE INDICATORS OF FIXED INVESTMENT**

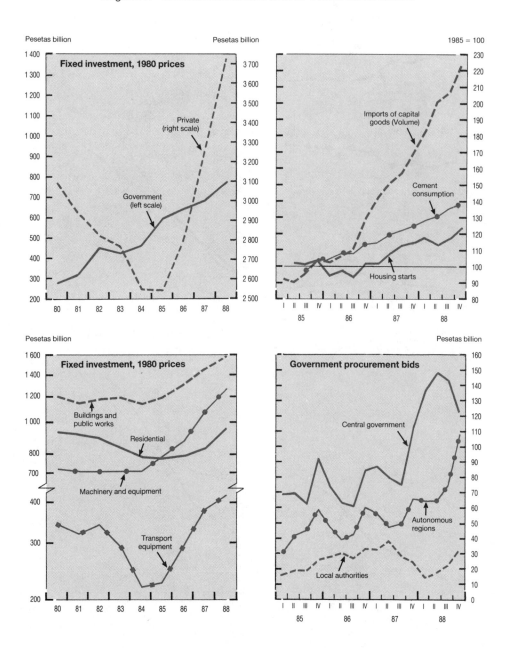

Sources: OECD, *National Accounts,* 1988; Boletín estadístico, Bank of Spain and OECD estimates.

Diagram 2. **PROFITS AND OPERATING SURPLUS**

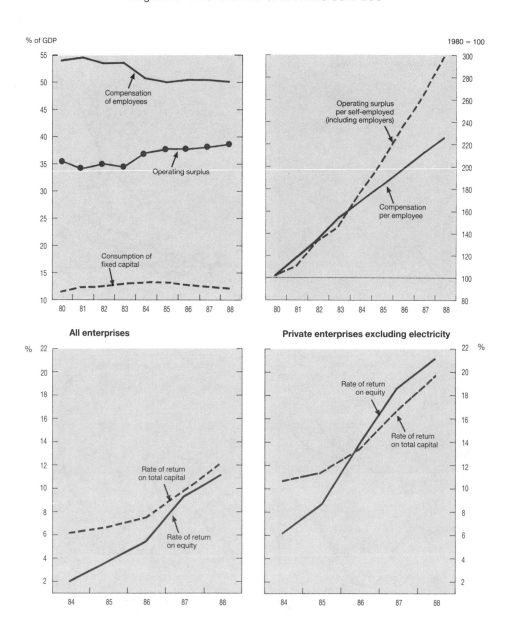

Sources: Central de Balances, Banco de España; OECD *National Accounts* and OECD estimates.

Table 2. **Pattern of output growth**

Percentage change over previous year

	1984	1985	1986	1987	1988 provisional
Agricultural output	8.6	3.1	−9.1	9.6	3.7
Non-agricultural output	1.3	2.3	4.2	5.3	5.0
Industry	1.1	2.1	5.6	5.1	4.2
Construction	−6.2	2.2	5.9	10.4	10.5
Services	2.7	2.3	3.4	4.8	4.6
Government	3.1	4.2	4.1	5.0	4.2
Private	2.5	1.9	3.2	4.7	5.0
GDP at market prices	1.8	2.3	3.3	5.5	5.0

Source : OECD, *National Accounts* and OECD estimates.

The contribution of stockbuilding to the growth of demand seems to have been small as involuntary inventory reductions have reportedly taken place in some capital goods industries. All in all, provisional estimates suggest that total aggregate demand rose by about 7 per cent in volume terms. As in 1987 an important part of this increase spilled over into imports of goods and services, which after having increased in volume terms by more than 20 per cent in 1987 rose by a further 15 per cent, more than twice the rate for exports.

Despite sizeable import leakages, GDP grew by 5 per cent in 1988, only slightly less than in 1987. The deceleration is virtually fully accounted for by the halving of the growth rate of agricultural production[4]. Reflecting the surge in investment, construction output grew twice as fast as GDP. Partial indicators suggest that the apparent slowdown in industrial production was due to mining. Manufacturing output increased by about 4¾ per cent for the third year running. Despite the steep upward trend in output, the margin of unused capacity changed little in 1988, except for capital goods industries. There was no change in the rate of growth of output of services, but for the first time in the 1980s private services expanded faster than general government.

Improved labour market conditions

The rapid growth of employment which, after a protracted period of subdued labour demand, began in the second half of 1985 and gathered momentum in 1987

15

Table 3. **Labour market**

Percentage change over previous year

	1984	1985	1986	1987	1988	1988 Q4
Total labour force	0.6	0.8	1.7	2.4	1.6	0.5
Total employment	−1.8	−0.9	2.2	3.1	2.9	2.5
of which:						
Excluding agriculture	−1.4	−0.6	4.9	4.2	3.7	3.5
Employees	−2.8	0.0	4.7	4.2	4.7	4.6
of which:						
Excluding agriculture	−3.9	−0.6	5.5	4.6	5.1	5.0
Unemployment rate (per cent)	(20.1)	(21.5)	(21.0)	(20.5)	(19.5)	(18.5)
Labour productivity, total[1]	3.5	3.3	0.9	2.3	2.0	..
Excluding agriculture	3.6	2.8	−0.7	1.0	1.4	..
of which:						
Manufacturing industry	3.2	5.8	3.5	3.4	2.6	..

1. Growth of the GDP at factor cost per employed.
Source: INE and *Síntesis Mensual de Indicadores Económicos*, Ministerio de Economía y Hacienda, Madrid 1989.

was sustained through 1988 (Table 3). While the agricultural labour force continued to shrink[5], almost 400 000 new jobs were created in other sectors, permitting a net increase in the number of employed people by 300 000 or 3 per cent of total employment. Reflecting the continued investment boom, employment growth in the construction sector was three times as high as the average. Employment in industry continued to expand at a lower rate than in services.

The rise in total employment was exclusively due to higher dependent employment, with employment in the public sector (including public enterprises) increasing by some 2.8 per cent[6] and the number of wage and salary earners in the non-agricultural private sector by 5 per cent. Female employment grew about twice as fast as male employment, in line with the trend established since the beginning of the upswing (Diagram 3). Increased job opportunities for women, notably in the service sector, have stimulated female labour supply. The female participation rate increased from an average of 29.3 per cent in the 1983-1985 period to 32.5 per cent in 1988, thereby offsetting the decline in male participation rates. Next to Ireland, female participation rates in Spain have, however, remained by far the lowest in the OECD area.

The creation of new jobs has been importantly helped by labour market measures[7]. Hirings under the Employment Promotion Programmes accounted for

16

Diagram 3. **EMPLOYMENT TRENDS**

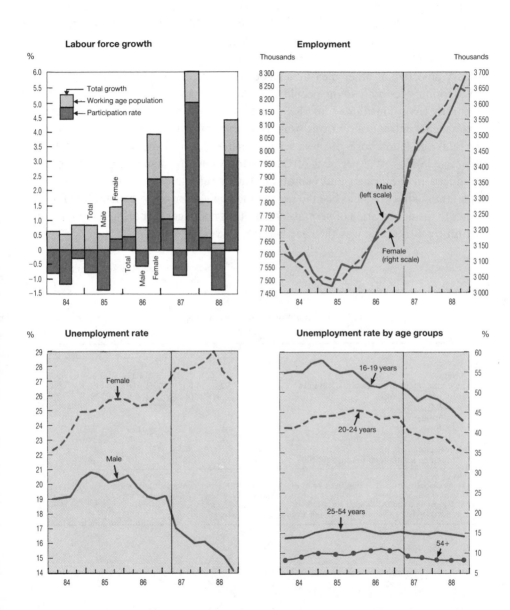

Sources: Boletín de Estadísticas Laborales, Ministerio de Trabajo y Seguridad Social and Síntesis Mensual de Indicadores Económicos, Ministerio de Economía y Hacienda.

17

54 per cent of total hirings of some 3.7 million in 1988, up from 27 per cent in 1984, i.e. prior to the extension of principal programmes (Table 4). The majority of these hirings were on the basis of temporary contracts and 14 per cent concerned part-time workers. These types of contracts have introduced a large degree of flexibility into the labour market, compensating in part for otherwise rigid hiring and lay-off rules. The primary objective of other measures has been the promotion of youth employment and of training for both young people and adults. In various ways all these measures appear to have contributed to the fact that an estimated half of these special employment contracts were transformed on termination into "permanent" contracts. The total budgetary costs of these schemes increased by some 40 per cent between 1986 and 1988, to 0.8 per cent of GDP. More recently, some changes have been introduced in the design and operation of some of these programmes. The most important modification has been to restrict the application of tax expenditure for new hirings to the net creation of *permanent* jobs, thus no longer favouring temporary and part-time contracts as was the case before[8].

Table 4. **Employment promotion programmes**

Thousands

	1984	1985	1986	1987	1988
Total hirings	1 830	2 571	3 020	3 449	3 712
Under employment promotion programmes	500	1 119	1 416	1 680	2 005
(Per cent of total hirings)	(27.4)	(43.5)	(46.9)	(48.7)	(54.0)
of which:					
Temporary contracts	235	432	537	667	862
Part-time	48	124	179	222	291
Training and apprenticeships	41	165	248	346	434
Youth employment[1]	–	56	104	119	
Agreements with government agencies[2]	101	270	309	293	293

1. Under 26 years of age.
2. Agreements between the National Institute of Employment (INEM) and government agencies, mainly local authorities and autonomous regions for employing (mainly in construction) registered unemployed persons.
Source: *Boletín de Estadísticas Laborales*, Ministerio de Trabajo y Seguridad Social, Madrid 1989 and *Síntesis Mensual de Indicadores Económicos*, Ministerio de Economía y Hacienda, Madrid 1989.

While it is difficult to say what the net employment effect of labour market measures has been, there can be little doubt that by having reduced current and fixed-cost elements of the use of labour, the creation of jobs has been favoured and that of low-productivity jobs most. In addition, by making labour input more adjustable to current production schedules and by stimulating demand and supply for part-time labour and temporary work, the trend decline of average working time per man-year has been reinforced, resulting in a deceleration in the growth of output per man. In fact, labour productivity advances (man-year) in non-agriculture since 1986 have not only dropped below the OECD average but have also been very modest (no more than half) relative to those recorded in previous cyclical upswings. If the weakish productivity growth were exclusively attributable to the government labour market measures and increased government employment with the level of overall output (heroically) assumed to be little affected, it could be argued that perhaps over one-third of the 1.2 million employment growth in non-agriculture since 1984 was in one way or the other the result of employment promotion and labour-market flexibility measures.

As the growth of the labour force slowed down somewhat in 1988, the rate of unemployment receded more than in 1987, dropping to 18½ per cent by the end of the year, though remaining the highest in the OECD area. Reflecting differentials in labour supply growth, the rate of male unemployment fell by 1.6 percentage points on average between 1987 and 1988, whereas the decline of female unemployment was negligible (from 28 per cent in 1987 to 27.7 per cent in 1988). Partly due to specific employment promotion schemes, the youth unemployment rate experienced the sharpest reduction, though to the still extremely high rate of 40 per cent, compared with 13½ per cent for the age group 25 to 64. Another encouraging feature is the reversal of the earlier steep upward trend in long-term unemployment (more than two years out of work). In the five years to 1987, its share in total unemployment had gone up by 15 percentage points to 44 per cent before starting to fall towards the end of that year.

The still very high level of unemployment after three years of strong demand and output growth must be seen against the background of a sharp acceleration of labour force growth from an annual rate of 1.2 per cent between 1982 and 1985 to 3 per cent during the following three years. With the growth of the working-age population remaining virtually unchanged, this acceleration reflected a turnaround in partici- pation rates. Reflecting discouraged-worker effects, the overall rate of participation had declined by 1.5 percentage points cumulatively during the three years preceding the economic upswing, before rising by 1 percentage point in the following three years. The added-labour effect associated with improved job opportunities is entirely attributable to increased female participation, as the male participation rate continued to decline by about 0.7 percentage points annually.

19

The pick-up of inflation

A major objective of the present Government has been to bring the rate of inflation into line with that of major trading partners, notably countries participating in the European Monetary System. To view this objective in a historical perspective Diagram 4 depicts Spain's relative inflation performance over the past two decades.

Diagram 4. **THE INTERNATIONAL PROCESS OF DISINFLATION**
Consumer prices, per cent change

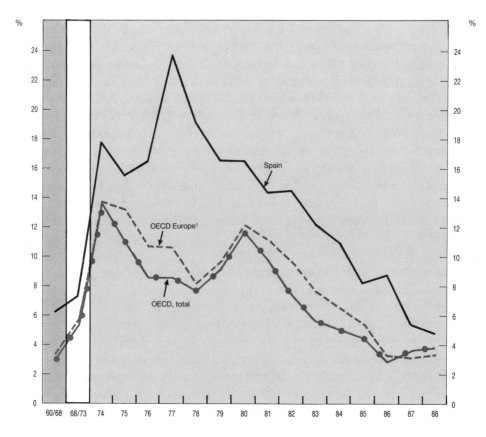

1. Excluding Turkey.
Source: OECD, *Economic Outlook.*

20

As can be seen, inflation as measured by the rise in the consumer price index has traditionally been high by international comparison. Starting with a small positive inflation differential at the beginning of the 1970s, the margin relative to the OECD average widened dramatically between the two oil shocks, peaking at almost 16 per cent in 1977. It then diminished equally fast to reach a low of 2.6 per cent in 1980 before attaining a new high of close to 7 per cent in 1983. Since then there has been a rather steady narrowing of the gap to no more than 1 per cent in 1988, only temporarily interrupted in 1986 by the introduction of the VAT which pushed the level of consumer prices up by an estimated 2 percentage points.

A closer look at the behaviour of major price components since 1984 suggests, however, that the disinflation process has been greatly aided by the trend decline of volatile food prices and, even more importantly, the fall of energy prices. As shown in Diagram 5 the annualised rise of the consumer price index, excluding food and energy and net of VAT effects, has been hovering around a stable trend rate of about 5½ per cent throughout the present upswing. The year-on-year rise of the overall index bottomed out at a low of less than 4 per cent in May 1988. Thereafter, reflecting less favourable price developments of food but possibly also the mounting pressure on resources in a few sectors, consumer prices reaccelerated, pushing the December index 5.8 per cent above its level of a year earlier.

The apparent stalling of the process of disinflation appears to reflect growing demand pressure rather than increased cost push. Indeed, as shown in Table 5 the upward pressure on unit labour costs continued to diminish as the rise of average earnings slowed down, while productivity advances remained broadly the same. As in previous years wage negotiations were guided by the government objective of bringing the year-on-year rate of consumer price inflation down to 3 per cent by December 1988. About three-quarters of wage contracts embodied clauses for pay adjustments in the event of higher-than-targeted prices. More than 3 500 agreements were concluded, covering some two-thirds of all employees, most of whom were on indefinite contracts. In the event, wage settlements exceeded somewhat government recommendations. At the same time, user costs of capital appear to have changed little given the fall in interest rates and stability of prices of imported capital goods. Finally, energy prices experienced a bigger fall on average than in 1987.

One reason why reduced cost push has not checked the inflation spiral can be found in the behaviour of non-energy import prices which, after a decline in 1986 and virtual stability in 1987, accelerated to almost 2.9 per cent in 1988. On the other hand, import prices of finished manufactures exhibited even greater stability than in previous years, which helps to explain why the price trend of industrial consumer goods continued to flatten throughout 1988.

Diagram 5. **UNDERLYING INFLATION**
Consumer prices, annualised rate of change over previous quarter

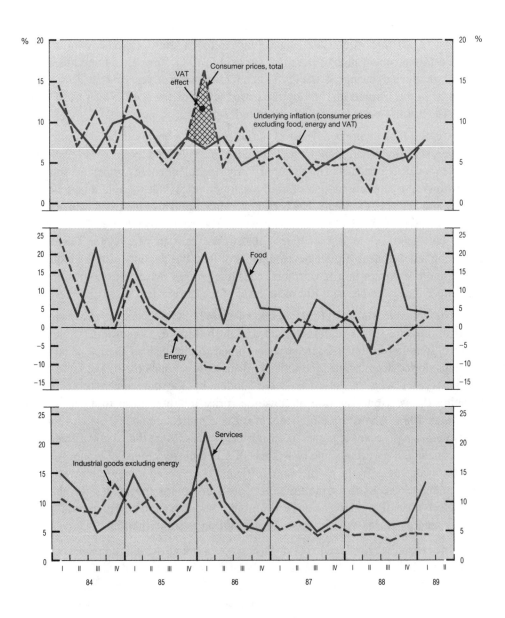

Sources: Boletín estadistico, Banco de España and OECD estimates.

Table 5. Wages and costs

Percentage change over previous year

	1985	1986	1987	1988	December 1987	December 1988
Collective wage agreements	7.9	8.2	6.5	5.3	6.5	5.3
Basic hourly pay	9.8	10.4	8.3	8.1	9.3	9.1
Average earnings[1]	9.7	11.3	7.0	6.0	7.8	6.1
Industry	11.0	11.9	7.7	5.9	9.4	6.2
Construction	4.6	11.0	4.9	3.5	−0.2	4.6
Services	7.8	10.6	6.4	7.0	6.4	6.3
Compensation per employee (national account basis)	8.5	8.2	7.3	6.3		
Government	8.6	8.4	6.7	6.3		
Private[2]	8.4	8.2	7.5	6.3		
Unit labour costs, total	5.2	7.2	5.1	4.3		
of which:						
Industry	4.8	5.0	3.9	3.5		

1. Growth of average earnings per month.
2. Private sector including companies owned or controlled by the general government.
Source: Síntesis Mensual de Indicadores Económicos, Ministerio de Economía y Hacienda, Madrid 1989 and Boletín de Estadísticas Laborales, Ministerio de Trabajo y Seguridad Social, Madrid 1989.

Table 6. Prices

Percentage change over previous year

	Weights	1985	1986	1987	1988	December 1987	December 1988	March 1989
Consumer prices, total	100.0	8.8	8.8	5.2	4.8	4.6	5.8	6.1
Food	33.0	9.5	10.6	5.0	3.7	2.7	6.4	6.4
Energy	7.0	4.4	−6.2	−3.9	−0.8	1.8	−2.1	−2.5
Other industrial goods	25.7	9.9	9.8	6.3	4.9	5.6	4.4	4.4
Services	34.2	8.4	9.1	6.3	6.8	6.3	7.6	8.8
Industrial prices, total	100.0	8.0	0.9	0.8	3.0	2.4	3.4	4.4[1]
Consumer goods	35.9	7.7	5.1	3.9	3.3	2.8	3.6	4.6
Capital goods	12.8	8.3	6.2	5.0	4.7	4.9	4.2	4.8
Intermediate goods	51.3	8.1	−3.1	−2.4	2.3	1.5	3.1	4.2
Agricultural prices received by farmers		2.0	8.8	−2.8	3.3	−5.7	10.8	
Cost of construction	100.0	8.8	4.8	4.1	5.5	5.1	6.9	
Buildings	75.0	8.9	5.4	4.5	5.6	5.1	7.1	
Public works	25.0	8.5	3.2	3.1	5.0	5.1	6.5	

1. February 1989 to February 1988 for industrial prices.
Source: Boletín estadístico, Bank of Spain, Madrid 1989.

Another reason for the stickiness of inflation would seem to lie in the behaviour of service prices. Reflecting buoyant demand and substantial increases in personal income, rent increases were higher than in 1987 and average earnings in services did not moderate as they did in other sectors. Even excluding rent, prices of services rose faster than average earnings, pointing to rising profit margins, professional fees and self-employment income. It is interesting to note in this context that the percentage difference between the rise of services (other than rents) and the consumer price index in total has been more than twice as big in recent years as in the OECD area as a whole.

Growing real and financial capital imports

Judged by the rise of foreign exchange reserves and the appreciation of the peseta in real and effective terms, the overall balance of payments has remained in a strong position throughout the period of present upswing (Table 7). The current balance, though benefiting from low oil prices and continued non-oil terms-of-trade gains, has moved into a growing deficit (on a seasonally-adjusted basis) since the second half of 1987, but the parallel surge of capital inflows, together with favourable trends in export earnings and current transfers have been more than sufficient to cover the steeply rising import bill.

The traditional trade deficit, which had doubled between 1986 and 1987, experienced another big jump in 1988. The deterioration was entirely due to volume changes as both total and non-energy terms of trade improved for the fifth year in succession. As shown in Diagram 6 unit labour costs relative to those in competitor countries measured in a common currency increased by almost 7 per cent in 1988, after an increase of close to 6 per cent in the preceding two years. The cumulative deterioration of cost competitiveness over the three years of more than 13 per cent is wholly due to unit labour costs (in local currency terms) rising faster in Spain than on average in trading partner countries. In 1988, according to OECD calculations, the peseta appreciated in effective terms by more than 3 per cent but this did not fully compensate for its continued downward slide in 1987 and 1986. Excluding food, the volume growth of exports of manufactured goods accelerated to nearly 9 per cent, broadly in line with export market growth. The deterioration in cost and price competitiveness appears thus to have been largely compensated for by the favourable trade creation effects arising from Spain's accession to the EC. Moreover, it is relevant to note that the level of Spanish labour costs is still considerably lower than the OECD average.

Table 7.   **Balance of payments**

Cash basis, $ billion

	1985	1986	1987	1988
Trade balance (fob/cif)	−5.9	−5.6	−11.4	−16.0
Exports	22.6	26.8	33.2	39.6
Imports	28.5	32.4	44.6	55.6
Non-factor services, net	8.2	11.5	13.1	12.8
of which :				
Tourism	7.1	10.5	12.8	14.2
Credits excluding tourism	5.4	6.1	7.0	7.5
Debits excluding tourism	4.4	5.2	6.7	8.9
Net investment income	−1.9	−2.0	−2.9	−3.5
Credit	1.6	1.5	3.0	4.1
Debit	3.5	3.5	5.9	7.6
Private transfers, net	1.4	1.5	2.5	3.7
Official transfers, net	−0.3	−0.4		
Invisible balance	7.5	10.6	12.7	13.0
Current balance	1.6	5.0	1.3	−3.0
Net long-term capital inflows	−1.7	−1.6	9.6	10.2
of which :				
Private foreign investments	2.5	5.2	8.0	9.1
Direct	1.0	2.0	2.6	4.5
Real estate	0.5	1.4	1.8	2.3
Portfolio	1.0	1.7	3.4	2.1
Credits from abroad	−2.7	−3.8	2.3	3.1
Basic balance	−0.1	3.4	10.9	7.2
Balance on non-monetary transactions[1]	0.1	3.1	11.6	5.9
Private monetary institutions, short-term capital	−1.9	−0.2	2.6	3.8
Change in offical reserves (+ = increase)	−1.9	2.7	14.2	9.7
Memorandum items :				
Transaction basis, fob/fob				
Trade balance	−4.5	−6.5	−12.9	−17.6
Invisible balance	7.0	10.4	12.8	14.0
Current account balance	2.5	3.9	0.0	−3.6
Gross external debt, end of period	28.6	24.5	30.6	33.0
Official reserves, end of period	13.3	16.0	30.2	39.9

1.   Including errors and omissions.
Source :   *Boletín estadístico*, Bank of Spain, Madrid 1989.

Import volumes again grew rapidly in 1988, albeit less than in 1987. The EC effects[9], together with losses in cost and price competitiveness, may explain two-fifths or even more of the 25 per cent growth of imports of food and manufactures, leaving the remainder to be explained by the buoyancy of domestic demand. The implied import-GDP elasticity of just over 2 is high both by international comparison and

Diagram 6. **EXCHANGE RATES AND INTERNATIONAL COMPETITIVENESS**

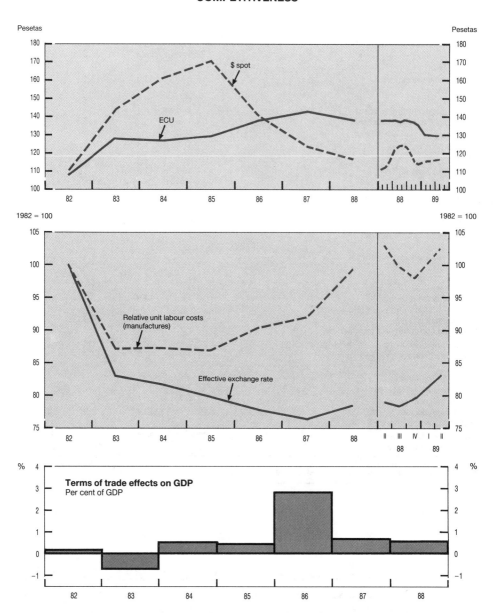

Sources: OECD, *Main Economic Indicators* and OECD estimates.

past experience, but should not be taken as indicative of a new trend. Apart from the fact that real domestic demand continued to grow much faster than potential output, the components of demand with the highest import content grew particularly fast. In fact, imports of machinery and equipment went up by 26 per cent in volume and transport equipment by as much as 44 per cent. These two items contributed two-thirds to the nominal increase in merchandise imports.

Though less marked than in previous years, the EC share in both exports and imports has continued to increase, reflecting both trade creation and diversion effects (Table 8). In 1988, the EC share in Spain's exports was higher than in other EC countries, whereas that in imports was somewhat lower[10]. This is an encouraging result as earlier evidence suggested[11] that the initial effects of Spain's EC entry would be asymmetric because the reaction lags on the export side were thought to be longer than on the import side. In this context it should also be noted that an important motivation behind large parts of foreign investments in recent years has been the aim of expanding Spain's export capacity to the rest of the EC. As to the foreign trade

Table 8. **Merchandise trade**

	Exports (f.o.b.)				Imports (c.i.f.)			
	Volume, percentage changes							
	1985	1986	1987	1988	1985	1986	1987	1988
Total	2.5	−4.3	6.9	6.2	7.0	16.6	22.2	13.9
Non-energy	1.7	−7.9	7.7	6.5	10.0	23.5	26.8	20.2
Food	−2.0	−2.2	17.0	−5.6	5.3	17.6	24.3	25.1
Raw materials	10.9	0.3	29.4	20.1	6.6	2.7	11.7	−4.0
Manufactures	2.1	−9.4	4.6	8.8	11.9	30.0	30.2	23.5
of which :								
Intermediate goods	3.4	−14.3	2.1	1.5	9.1	37.2	14.7	14.8
Capital goods	2.0	−10.1	7.7	24.9	13.6	18.1	39.3	29.1
Consumer goods	0.6	−3.8	5.6	8.0	14.1	36.9	41.3	27.2
	Percentage shares in total							
OECD	70.2	77.4	79.5	80.9	56.8	71.6	73.9	77.3
USA	10.0	9.2	8.1	7.9	10.9	9.9	8.3	8.9
OECD Europe	57.5	65.5	68.8	70.3	41.6	55.7	60.0	62.4
EEC	52.3	60.4	63.8	65.6	36.8	50.3	54.6	56.7
Other	2.7	2.7	2.5	2.7	4.3	6.0	5.6	6.0
OPEC	7.2	5.6	4.6	4.5	20.1	11.3	9.5	6.7
Latin America	5.1	4.8	3.5	3.1	10.6	6.8	6.0	5.2
Comecon	2.9	1.8	1.6	1.3	2.4	1.8	2.6	2.6
Other	14.6	10.5	10.8	10.1	10.1	8.6	8.0	8.2

Source : *Síntesis Mensual de Indicadores Económicos*, Ministerio de Economía y Hacienda, Madrid 1989.

shares of non-EC countries, it can be seen that except for Comecon all other major groups of countries lost market shares in Spain during the last few years and that similar declines have occurred on the export side with shrinking export volumes to the depressed Latin American and Comecon markets for three years in a row.

The increase in the 1988 trade deficit (fob/cif) to 6 per cent of GDP was partly offset by a rise in the traditional surplus on invisibles. Net transfers from the EC trebled to just over $1 billion and net tourist receipts again increased markedly despite a steep trend rise of Spanish tourist expenditure abroad (some 20 per cent, annual rate, since 1986). After remaining broadly stable between 1983 and 1987, payments for other services also grew rapidly, turning the traditional surplus on non-tourism services into deficit. This turnaround reflects the opening of the Spanish economy and the concomitant increase in commissions, royalties, fees, etc. and to a lesser extent higher freight and insurance costs as a result of the rapid expansion of

Table 9.   **Saving and investment balances**
Per cent of GDP

	1980-84 average	1985	1986	1987	1988
Private saving	19.6	21.9	21.9	20.4	20.9
Household	8.6	8.5	8.1	7.9	8.2
Business	11.0	13.4	13.8	12.5	12.7
Government saving	−0.1	−1.4	−0.5	1.4	1.8
Total domestic saving (gross)	19.4	20.4	21.5	21.8	22.7
Investment (gross)	21.0	18.8	19.8	21.8	23.8
Foreign saving[1]	1.5	−1.6	−1.7	0.0	1.1
of which :					
Foreign long-term investment	1.0	1.5	2.2	2.8	2.7
of which :					
Direct business and real estate investment	0.9	1.2	1.5	1.5	2.0
Memorandum item :					
Net lending[2], total	−1.6	1.6	1.8	0.3	−0.9
Private sector	2.9	8.6	7.8	3.9	2.3
Household	3.1	3.8	3.9	4.1	3.5
Business	−0.2	4.8	3.9	−0.2	−1.2
Government	−4.5	−7.0	−6.1	−3.6	−3.2

1.   Foreign savings is equal to the current external balance with the opposite sign.
2.   Total net lending indicates increases (minus sign) in foreign net liabilities of Spain, equal to the current external balance less net capital transfers. Net lending of the individual sectors show changes in net liabilities (net assets) vis-à-vis both foreign and resident sectors.
Source :   OECD *National Accounts* and OECD estimates.

trade. Finally, and not surprisingly, net payments on interest, dividends and profits grew briskly, reflecting the rapid build-up of a large stock of foreign capital in Spain[12].

Net long-term capital inflows amounted to some $10 billion in 1988, up from $9 billion in 1987. The major part of this inflow was accounted for by direct investments in both business and in real estate. Portfolio investment also remained strong, in part also reflecting increased foreign participation in Spanish firms and capital injections into own companies. All in all, direct capital inflows into business and real estate might therefore have amounted to some $7 billion in 1988 or 2 per cent of GDP, equal to more than twice the current account deficit[13]. Financial capital movements of a largely short-term nature, provoked by wide interest-rate differentials, also generated large inflows, more than offsetting the big surge of Spanish foreign capital investments and commercial credits to foreigners.

The marked changes which have occurred in the structure of the balance of payments over the past three years of rapid growth can best be assessed if viewed against the associated changes in domestic saving and investment levels and sectoral financial balances. As can be seen from Table 9 domestic savings in terms of gross national income shares rose from 20.4 per cent in 1985 to 22.7 per cent in 1988, somewhat above the OECD average. The rise was exclusively due to a marked swing in the general government sector account from negative to positive saving, which more than offset the apparent 1988 drop in private sector savings. At the same time, the gross investment ratio rose even more steeply, by almost 5 per cent of GDP in the three years to 1988, necessitating a net recourse to foreign savings to the tune of 1 per cent of GDP. As noted above, the actual transfer of funds has not, so far, posed any problem. In fact, the capital attracted to Spain by the prospect of high rates of return was, if anything, over-abundant, putting excessive upward pressure on the peseta and complicating monetary management.

II. Economic policies and short-term prospects

With the economy in its third year of boom, economic policy-making has become increasingly difficult. While the maintenance of sufficient growth to improve labour market conditions has continued to top the list of government priorities, the surrounding conditions for keeping the rapidly growing economy on an even keel have become less favourable. First, with the international process of disinflation coming to an end, the strong disinflationary impact from abroad on Spanish prices has diminished. Secondly, the extra room for demand expansion provided to the economy at the start of the upswing by a comfortable current balance-of-payments surplus has been gradually exhausted. Thirdly, after three years of strong output growth, supply bottlenecks have emerged in certain sectors of the economy. Fourthly, in accordance with the government's supply-side-oriented strategy towards output and employment growth, labour has so far shown an appreciably high degree of wage moderation, thereby actively supporting the official stabilisation policy and the restructuring process. This has, however, led to marked changes in the distribution of income, increasing trade union militancy for higher pay and social benefits, and, more generally, weakening the basis for social consensus.

Fiscal policy

The much stronger-than-anticipated growth of output and prices in 1988 led, according to OECD estimates, to a significantly steeper rise in general government tax revenues than officially projected[14] (Table 10). Particularly rapid was the increase in direct tax receipts, above all taxes on personal incomes[15]. The effects of fiscal drag[16] and the efforts made to curb tax evasion more than compensated for the tax losses associated with reforms in personal income taxation[17]. Rising profits and the decrease in business tax allowances from 15 to 10 per cent of investment expenditure boosted corporate tax receipts.

Table 10. **General government accounts**
National accounts definitions
Pesetas billion

	1985	1986	1987	1988
Current revenue	9 615	11 189	13 092	14 452
Direct taxes	2 378	2 638	3 657	4 095
Indirect taxes	2 686	3 412	3 680	4 048
Social security contributions	3 660	4 142	4 624	5 058
Other	891	977	1 131	1 251
Current expenditure	10 173	11 538	12 817	14 036
Public consumption	3 907	4 470	5 142	5 671
of which :				
Wages and salaries	2 975	3 339	3 719	4 157
Social security benefits	4 151	4 655	5 170	5 686
Interest payments	900	1 202	1 252	1 314
Current transfers and other	1 215	1 211	1 253	1 365
Net saving	−558	−349	275	416
(% of GDP)	(−2.0)	(−1.1)	(0.8)	(1.1)
Consumption of fixed capital	169	194	241	300
Fixed investment[1]	1 045	1 179	1 268	1 490
Net capital transfer payments	523	606	549	499
Net lending (+) or net borrowing (−)	−1 957	−1 940	−1 301	−1 273
(% of GDP)	(−7.0)	(−6.1)	(−3.6)	(3.2)
Memorandum items :				
Changes in financial balances (per cent of GDP)[2]				
Actual	(−1.5)	(+0.9)	(+2.4)	(+0.4)
Built-in stabilizers	(−0.4)	(+0.2)	(+1.0)	(+0.9)
Structural balance, total	(−1.1)	(+0.7)	(+1.4)	(−0.5)

Note : Because of rounding figures may not add up to total.
1. Including purchase of land.
2. Changes in net lending; a positive sign indicates a move towards restriction (surplus) and a negative sign a move towards expansion (deficit).
Sources : OECD *National Accounts* and OECD estimates.

As often in the past, the extra tax receipts were in part used to finance additional expenditure. Central government investment and capital transfers rose particularly rapidly, with the latter being boosted by EC transfers[18]. By contrast, government consumption grew broadly in line with initial plans, implying a small fall in relation to GDP. The continuing rapid increase in government employment was partly offset by moderate pay rises for most categories of civil servants[19]. The growth of social security transfers also slowed down, partly due to improved labour-market conditions and rapidly increasing household income.

31

The cyclically-adjusted (structural) general government deficit increased further, but thanks to powerful built-in stabilisers the deficit (on a national accounts basis) declined to nearly 3 per cent of GDP in 1988, only marginally higher than had been projected. With the deficit being smaller than interest payments, a primary surplus was recorded for the first time since 1984. Including the acquisition of financial assets – mainly capital injections and credit to State-controlled companies and institutions – the total borrowing requirement fell to just below 4½ per cent of GDP[20]. Treasury bills continued to be the main financing instrument[21]. As in 1987, there was a net decrease in Treasury notes held by the non-bank public, reflecting their reduced attractiveness as a "tax haven". The State also repaid some of its debt to the Bank of Spain and the share of medium-term government bonds (maturity period of less than three years) in total government financing was increased slightly. The heavy reliance on short- to medium-term debt poses a number of problems for monetary management since the three-month repurchase agreements make medium-term debt instruments almost as liquid as short-term debt. In order to have a more balanced debt structure the government has decided to resume the issue of long-term bonds, starting with an issue of a ten-year bond in January 1989.

The consolidated Central Government Budget for 1989 (Table 11) provided for an increase in personal income tax allowances of about 3 per cent, leaving tax brackets unchanged[22]. However, in February 1989 the Court declared unconstitutional the obligation for families to cumulate taxable income implying higher marginal tax rates for second or third persons' incomes. The Government has announced that it will present a new fiscal law taking into account the Court's decision. In the meantime, it decided not to increase the income tax allowances by 3 per cent in 1989, as originally planned, so as to make good the tax shortfalls resulting from the Court's decision. Both income tax declarations and tax returns are likely to be delayed by about three months, i.e. until the new fiscal law is passed. All in all, tax receipts in 1989 are likely to be only marginally affected by the Court's decision. Fiscal drag and a further drive against evasion, especially to cover undeclared incomes invested in the past few years in a special life insurance scheme (primas unicas), are expected to lead to a sharp acceleration in personal income tax receipts in 1989[23]. Similarly, buoyant profits and a further reduction of the tax deduction for investments to 5 per cent of investment expenditure should result in a continuing rapid growth of corporate tax receipts. The increase in current revenues is expected to be considerably faster than that of current expenditure, implying a further sharp rise in central government saving. The wage and salary bill is estimated to rise by 10 per cent, with average earnings contributing nearly two-thirds and the increase in employment the rest. Social expenditure is planned to increase by some

Table 11. **State Budget and financing**

Cash basis, pesetas billion

	1985	1986	1987	1988		1989
				Budget	Outcome[1]	Budget
Total revenues	4 420	5 692	7 038	7 296	7 914	8 737
Direct taxes	1 947	2 167	3 156	3 107	3 518	4 003
of which:						
Households	1 544	1 641	2 490	2 383	2 714	3 006
Enterprises	403	526	666	724	804	997
Indirect taxes	1 833	2 781	3 159	3 296	3 513	3 751
Transfers	189	218	265	212	197	338
Other revenues	451	526	458	680	686	645
Total expenditure	5 883	7 073	8 318	8 625	9 030	9 896
Consumption	1 413	1 749	1 887	1 993	2 026	2 211
of which:						
Wages and salaries	1 224	1 520	1 585	1 728	1 738	1 898
Goods and services	189	229	302	265	288	313
Current transfers	2 568	3 187	4 134	4 175	4 378	4 733
Interest payments	700	1 065	994	993	1 166	1 120
Fixed investment	450	382	601	653	618	911
Capital transfers	749	689	695	811	842	921
Other	3	1	7	..	..	..
Budget balance	−1 463	−1 381	−1 280	−1 329	−1 116	−1 159
Extra budgetary operations	−27	−65	−54	..	−56	..
Net overall balance	−1 490	−1 446	−1 334	−1 329	−1 172	−1 159
Financial operations, net	−49	−17	−87	−68	−279	−405
Borrowing requirement	−1 539	−1 463	−1 421	−1 397	−1 591	−1 564
Financing net:						
Short-term debt[2]	1 136	937	1 715		916	
Medium and long-term debt	271	1 650	298		948	
Bank of Spain	442	−607	−314		−342	
Other	−310	−517	−278		−71	

Memorandum items:

Deficit, national accounts basis (per cent of GDP)	1985	1986	1987	1985	1986	1987
	Gross deficit			Net of intra-government transfers		
General government	7.0	6.1	3.6	7.0	6.1	3.6
State	6.1	5.3	3.6	0.1	−1.0	−2.5
Autonomous organisations	0.0	0.0	0.0	0.9	0.3	0.2
Social security	0.3	0.1	−0.2	4.3	4.2	4.3
Territorial governments	0.6	0.7	0.2	1.7	2.5	1.6

Note: Because of rounding figures may not add up to total.

1. Official estimates.
2. Short-term debt includes Treasury notes and bills.
Sources: Intervención General; Presentación de los Presupuestos Generales del Estado 1989, Ministerio de Economia y Hacienda; OECD estimates.

12 per cent, mainly due to the continuous steep growth in health expenditure and the number of pensioners. Reflecting the improved profit situation in public enterprises, capital transfers are forecast to decline. Partly supported by EC funds fixed investment is again budgeted to increase rapidly – by over one-third – mainly to improve the infrastructure.

The budgeted small decrease in the Central Government deficit is likely to be broadly offset by an increase in the deficit of the Autonomous Regions and Local Authorities. After the Consolidated Central Government Budget was voted, expenditure appropriations for pensions and unemployment benefits were increased to the tune of ½ per cent of GDP to be compensated for by spending cuts elsewhere. Moreover, the recent sharp increase in interest rates might raise interest payments by about ½ per cent of GDP. On the other hand, as discussed below, output, prices and household incomes can be expected to grow considerably faster than assumed, reinforcing built-in stabilisers. In total, and allowing for usual expenditure overruns (see Part III), the general government deficit may decline to below 3 per cent of GDP. In addition, as in the previous few years, substantial financial investments are planned, so that total borrowing requirements can be expected to exceed 4 per cent of GDP.

Monetary policy

In the face of the unexpected strength of the economy, continuous huge capital inflows, encouraged since 1986 by the liberalisation of capital imports[24], and with reaccelerating inflation in the second half of last year, monetary management has become increasingly difficult. On the one hand, with interest-rate levels significantly exceeding the rate of growth of national income and international competitiveness being eroded by persistently strong upward pressure on the peseta, a policy conducive to a general lowering of interest-rate levels was thought desirable. On the other hand, in order to make good the diminishing disinflation impetus from abroad, a tightening of the monetary policy stance was called for. Since late-summer 1988, the Bank of Spain has decided to tip the balance in favour of the latter course, partly also with a view to compensating for the continued expansionary effects of fiscal policy.

Throughout 1988 total demand for credit remained strong, entailing an overshooting of initial targets for the public and especially the private sector. Domestic credit to households and business increased by 16 per cent compared with 11 per cent originally planned (Table 12). Particularly strong was the credit

Table 12. **Monetary aggregates**

Pesetas billion, end of month

	1988	1985	1986	1987	1988	February 1989
	Pesetas billion	Annual percentage change				
Currency	3 241	11.8	15.4	13.9	18.5	19.8
Sight deposits	6 467	17.1	11.9	15.8	17.5	19.2
M1	9 708	12.0	13.0	15.1	17.8	19.4
Savings deposits	7 244	10.9	12.7	7.6	12.7	12.4
Time deposits	10 393	−0.5	−6.0	2.4	2.7	2.9
M3	27 345	5.4	3.9	7.7	10.3	10.6
Government liabilities	6 456	216.0	61.6	52.2	16.4	23.9
of which:						
Repurchase agreements	5 474	384.9	71.1	61.2	26.4	35.3
Private-created liquid assets	2 888	21.5	55.6	11.7	−1.3	−4.5
Other liquid assets	9 344	87.7	59.1	35.3	10.3	14.1
ALP[1]	36 689	12.9	12.2	13.6	10.3	11.5
ALP target		11.5-14.5	9.5-12.5	6.5-9.5	8.0-11.0	6.5-9.5
Net domestic credit to residents	41 657	14.8	13.0	13.7	14.6	15.9
Public sector	13 627	35.8	23.3	13.7	11.9	14.4
Private sector	28 030	7.4	8.4	13.8	16.0	16.6
GDP at market value	39 618	11.0	14.6	11.8	10.9	

1. ALP stands for "liquid assets in the hands of the public", which includes M3, Treasury Bills, repurchase operations with public assets, bank bonds, mortgage securities, bankers' acceptances, guaranteed commercial paper, liabilities on insurance operations, repurchase operations with private assets.
Source: Boletín estadístico, Banco de España, Madrid 1989.

expansion to households and to trading and construction sectors. Domestic credit to industry expanded comparatively little, reflecting both improved cash-flow and easier access to foreign loans at lower interest rates.

The wide money supply aggregate, ALP, for which the authorities had set a growth target range of 8 to 11 per cent for 1988, was just held within this range, contrary to developments in the preceding year when targets were overshot by a large margin. Financial innovations continued to influence the composition of ALP, but less than in previous years, when major changes in the financing of the government deficit took place. In 1988 sight deposits rose sharply, while the growth of time-deposits slowed down markedly. The steep increase in sight deposits, concentrated in the first few months, is largely attributable to the 1987 permission for banks to pay interest for sight deposits in line with the interest-rate deregulation policy.

Interest rates fluctuated considerably less in 1988 than in 1987, in part reflecting a smoother pattern of ALP growth and government borrowing and, as discussed above, increasing resort to more normal financing instruments (Diagram 7). Moreover, the initially strong impact of earlier financial liberalisation measures has

Diagram 7. **INTEREST RATES**

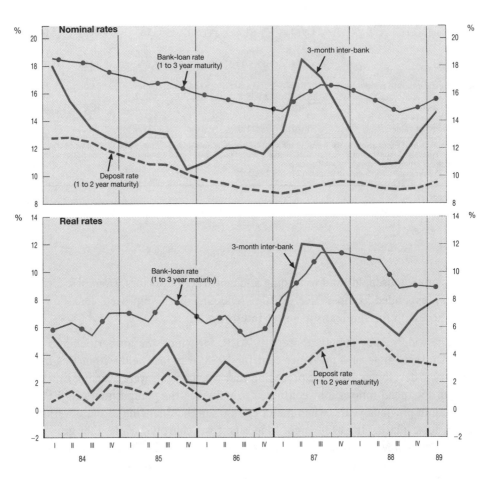

Source: OECD, *Financial Statistics*.

36

been petering out (see OECD, *Economic Survey of Spain*, January 1988). The Bank of Spain's aim of supporting real growth – as long as the disinflation process continued, if only modestly – and of checking further sizeable inflows of short-term capital from abroad was reflected in the downward trend of interest rates up to September. The official intervention rate fell by nearly 3 percentage points between the end of 1987 and August 1988, accompanied by a decline of 1½ percentage points in financial institutions' long-term lending rates. In response to the pick-up of inflation in the summer months, the intervention rate was raised in early September, followed by a significantly milder rise in financial institutions' lending rates. Even so, demand for credit further strengthened in the last quarter of 1988. At the same time, the widening of the already-large interest-rate differential provoked further capital inflows.

The liberalisation since mid-1987 of loans over one year from abroad, combined with improved facilities of exchange-risk cover, has led to sizeable inflows of financial credits. Benefiting from low foreign interest rates, borrowing from abroad (including bond placements) exceeded $600 million per month in the first half of 1988. At the same time, foreigners invested large amounts in Treasury bills and State bonds as well as in deposits of convertible pesetas. The rules barring the payment of interest for convertible peseta deposits exceeding 10 million Pesetas were not fully effective. Meanwhile, foreign capital inflows for direct investment in business and real estate continued their upward trend. In order to moderate the resulting pressure on the peseta and to reduce the costly intervention of sterilising part of these capital inflows, the monetary authorities raised the minimum period for financial borrowing from abroad to three years in June 1988. In subsequent months many maturing debts were not renewed resulting in a net capital outflow. However, financial and commercial net capital inflows have resumed since November, thereby further inflating overall liquidity and augmenting unrest in the foreign-exchange market.

In early February 1989, concerned about renewed inflation pressure, the monetary policy stance was tightened significantly, leading to a new round of interest-rate increases. In order to curb credit expansion financial institutions' non-interest-bearing cash deposits with the Bank of Spain were raised by 1.5 percentage points to 6.5 per cent[25] of eligible liabilities. Complementary measures were also taken in order to check capital inflows: 30 per cent of new financial borrowing from abroad (i.e. including new bond issues but excluding refinancing of existing loans and bonds) by commercial and industrial firms will have to be deposited in non-interest bearing deposits with the Bank of Spain and 20 per cent for new borrowing of financial institutions. Moreover, the Bank of Spain tightened controls over short-term capital inflows and in March a law was passed imposing a withholding tax on Treasury bills held by foreigners. The objective is to reduce the rate of growth of ALP to within the target range of 6.5 to 9.5 per cent set for 1989 and to ease upward pressure on the peseta. The Bank of Spain intervention rate gradually rose to 14 per cent and bank lending rates reached 17 per cent by mid-April. Adjusted for current inflation, the latter is one of the highest rates in the OECD area. These measures eased only moderately the upward pressure on the peseta and after continuing rapid growth in the first two months of 1989 (14.7 per cent, annual rate) the rate of increase of ALP slowed down to 5.8 per cent, annual rate, in March.

Structural policies

The past eighteen months have seen a continuation of industrial policies initiated in the mid-1980s. Since the early-1980s, industrial policy has aimed at improving the balance-sheet position of public firms (notably the INI group), and assisting the restructuring of industries most affected by the recession. As can be seen from Table 13 the profit situation of the INI group has improved markedly. In 1987 the overall losses of the group were reduced to a fifth, and first preliminary estimates suggest that the INI group may show an operating surplus for 1988 of the order of Ptas. 30 billion, almost 0.1 per cent of GDP. Twenty-seven firms of the group recorded profits, notably IBERIA (airline company), ENCE (paper pulp) and ENDESA (electricity supply). Thirty-three companies still made losses, notably CASA, the public aircraft company, although it reduced its losses by one-half in 1988. Own-equity finance represented only a quarter of total liabilities of the group in 1987, a slight improvement relative to previous years. Profits before interest

Table 13. **Results and indebtedness of the INI group**

In per cent of net assets

	1983	1984	1985	1986	1987
Profits before interest payments[1]	1.3	2.1	3.0	3.9	6.2
Profits after interest payments[1]	−8.7	−6.4	−5.2	−4.6	−1.7
Indebtedness	60.8	63.0	59.8	62.3	57.4
Memorandum item:					
Workforce (1983=100)	100	95.2	91.5	89.4	86.2

1. Profits include government subsidies and other transfers, for which no consolidated data exist.
Source: INI, Annual Report, 1987.

payments amounted to 6.2 per cent of net assets in 1987, 5 percentage points higher than in 1983 (Table 13); but after interest payments, the INI group as a whole still recorded losses totalling 1.7 per cent of net assets in 1987, compared to 8.7 per cent in 1983. Productivity gains through cuts in employment, a selective investment policy and better management, have been crucial factors behind the improvement. Employment fell by 14 per cent cumulatively between 1983 and 1987. Looking ahead, efficiency might be further enhanced by widening the capital base of INI firms by increasing private shareholding, but this process has not yet been sufficiently developed. The first public issue of (minority) shares was made in 1986. The biggest transaction took place in 1988, when ENDESA placed about a fifth of its shares in the capital market.

As discussed in the two previous OECD Surveys of Spain, an extensive programme for the reconversion of the industrial sector was launched in 1984. It aimed at enhancing competitiveness via adjustments to capacity and associated cuts in the workforce, financial restructuring and technological modernisation, supported by subsidies and public credits. Measures have been taken to limit the social consequences for workers and the regions most affected by the reconversion programme. By the end of 1987, 85 per cent of the envisaged cuts in employment had been made (Table 14). In a few sectors (electronic components for cars, fertilisers and shipbuilding) the cuts even exceeded initial plans. However, in other sectors the objectives had not been achieved, notably for STANDARD (telecommunications

Table 14. **Industrial restructuring programme**

	Reference period	Initial workforce	Target reduction	Actual reduction end-1987	Actual reduction in per cent of target
		Thousands			
Shipbuilding	1984-87	37 347	13 105	13 837	105.6
Carbon-based steel	1981-90	42 837	20 076	15 701	78.2
Speciality steel	1981-88	13 744	8 728	7 082	81.1
Home appliances	1981-88	23 869	12 611	11 544	89.1
Textiles	1982-86	108 844	9 925	9 925	100.0
Standard-ITT	1984-91	16 133	8 377	2 799	33.4
Electrical equipment	1982-85	6 720	1 342	1 451	108.1
Electronic components	1982-85	3 744	1 544	1 430	92.6
Others		27 173	7 280	6 821	98.4
Total		280 411	82 988	70 590	85.1

Source: Ministry of Industry, *Informe sobre la industria española*, 1987.

and equipment company) for which the period of reference has been extended by three years[26]. The degree of realisation of investment targets has been fairly high (80 per cent). Subsidies and credits by the Industrial Credit Bank, were equivalent to some 85 per cent of total investment undertaken by reconversion firms. The steel and textile industries were the main beneficiaries, receiving about 55 per cent of subsidies and more than 60 per cent of public credits.

Fiscal advantages, subsidies and public credits have been provided to create the ZUR's (zones for urgent reindustrialisation) in those areas most affected by the industrial restructuring programme. The target for job-creation was 23 000 (Table 15), and realisation so far 50 per cent. Investment plans have been more ambitious, but realisations have not been speedier. The ZUR's have been relatively costly in budgetary terms, as for each new job, Ptas.2.1 million were given by way of subsidy (almost twice the annual average wage). Even so, the cost-effectiveness of the ZURs in terms of employment-creation is officially estimated to be better than traditional regional policies.

Table 15. **Costs and benefits of the zones for urgent reindustrialisation**
1985-1988

	Projects approved	Realisation
Fixed investment (billion pesetas)	321	172
Employment (thousands)	23.3	11.8
Subsidies (millions of pesetas per employee)	2.1	—

Source: Ministry of Industry, *Informe sobre la industria española,* 1987.

A new law in defence of competition has recently been passed. It enlarges the domain of the previous law and improved its application. Under the old regime, only negative effects arising from agreements between firms gave rise to legal action but not the agreements themselves. In contrast, the new law renders illegal both agreements and practices which might distort competition, notably with respect of pricing, production and investment controls and marketing of products. Abuses of dominant market positions are also subject to legal investigations. However, there are circumstances where the Court can allow deviation from free competition, notably in cases of recession or of "excessive" competition from abroad.

The application of competition laws has been extended. Under the previous regime, the Court had limited powers. It could only make proposals to the administration which in the event could impose penalties. But since 1963, such a case had only arisen once. Under the new regime the Court is allowed to impose penalties on firms and is likely to make actual use of its power, being less exposed to political pressure and lobbying. However, a number of practices which are also liable to affect competition negatively are not covered by the new law. For instance, the damaging effects on competition stemming from concentration or public aid cannot be taken up by the Court. In these cases it can only give advice to the Government on necessary action to be taken.

Following Spain's accession to the EC and in response to favourable overall balance-of-payments developments, important restrictions to capital movements have been removed. As regards capital exports, direct business investments abroad have been wholly liberalised. Operations in quoted foreign-currency-denominated bonds and shares have also been liberalised, if carried out through designated financial institutions and if deposited in Spain. Real-estate operations abroad still require administrative clearance, but are no longer subject to quantitative ceilings. As to capital imports, all restrictions on direct investment, including real estate, and on the acquisition of securities quoted in the Spanish stock markets have been lifted except for operations in certain strategic sectors (defence, communications and air transport). However, as noted above, various temporary restrictions were reimposed recently to avoid excessive capital inflows.

Short-term prospects

Key assumptions

Given the momentum of growth experienced by most OECD economies over the past eighteen months or so, world trade can be expected to continue to expand at a healthy rate, at least through the current year. According to OECD's projections of last autumn, Spanish export markets for manufactured goods may expand by 7½ per cent in 1989, and around 7 per cent in 1990, after 8¾ per cent in 1988. The continuing worsening in cost competitiveness may be more than offset by some EC trade creation effects and increased export capacity so that some gains in market shares could well be made. On the assumption of unchanged exchange rates, import prices are projected to show a moderate acceleration over the next two years, except for prices of primary non-oil commodities where prospects are for a significant deceleration relative to developments in 1988.

As discussed in more detail above, fiscal policy can be expected to remain a mixture of demand-stimulating measures and demand-damping influences, the latter arising from powerful automatic stabiliser effects. On present plans, discretionary policy action embodied in the 1989 Budget is equivalent to an initial demand stimulus of about ½ per cent of GDP, the same as in 1988. Monetary policy will again carry the brunt of price stabilisation efforts. The severe measures taken in February should moderate the pace of monetary expansion and ease inflation pressure in the course of the year. Yet, due to policy-induced substitution of domestic for foreign credit and higher-than-expected nominal income growth, the target range for ALP growth of 6½ to 9½ per cent may be difficult to achieve.

The outlook for 1989-90

Following some slowing of activity around the middle of 1988, the economic expansion regathered strength towards the end of the year. The fall in unemployment became more pronounced in the last quarter of 1988 and a further decrease was recorded in the early months of this year. Inflation, measured by the rise of the consumer price index, edged up to 6.1 per cent on a year-on-year basis in March 1989. Recent foreign trade data also suggest that the expansion has acquired renewed momentum, which the rise in interest rates has so far failed to arrest[27]. In the first three months of 1989, the credit expansion to the private sector was at 17 per cent, annual rate, significantly stronger than a year earlier, with ALP growth rising at an annual rate of about 13 per cent.

Further developments through 1989 will in an important measure depend on the outcome of current wage negotiations. The Government has again set the norm for pay rises in 1989 at about 5 per cent. In view of greater trade union militancy and the failure of the Government to achieve last year's target, the growth of average earnings is assumed to accelerate to some 7½ per cent in 1989[28]. This, together with weaker price-damping influences from abroad would, taken by itself, make for stronger inflation pressure. However, non-accommodating monetary policy could contain this pressure, in particular if combined with further trade liberalisation and deregulation measures. In the present projections, presented below, it is assumed that consumer-price inflation will pick up somewhat in 1989 taken as a whole, but should ease off thereafter.

Though somewhat weaker than in 1988, fixed investment should remain the mainstay of the expansion (Table 16). Including a projected growth of some 12¾ per cent in 1989, fixed investment is expected to exceed its 1984 cyclical trough by about two-thirds, with its share in nominal GDP rising from 18¾ per cent to 23¾ per cent. Government investment is again projected to increase considerably faster than private investment, whose trend has begun to weaken. According to medium-term government plans, investment in infrastructure should show a sharp rise, with all levels of government evenly contributing[29]. Residential construction is expected to be adversely affected by the recent interest-rate hike and the abolition of tax rebates for the purchase of a second house, though the large backlog of orders and buildings under construction should limit the extent of the slowdown.

The effects of projected slower growth of employment on household incomes should be partly offset by a significant rise in real wage earnings and interest income.

Table 16. **The short-term outlook**

Annual percentage change

	1988[1]	1989	1990
	OECD projections		
Private consumption	4.6	4½	3¾
Government consumption	5.0	4	4
Gross fixed investment	14.0	12¾	9
Total domestic demand	7.0	6¼	5
Exports of goods and services	6.3	5¾	5½
Imports of goods and servics	15.2	12	9
Foreign balance[2]	−2.1	−1¾	−1¼
GDP at constant prices	5.0	4¾	4
of which :			
Manufacturing output	4.2	4	3¾
Memorandum items :			
Real household disposable income	4.7	4½	4
Compensation per employee, private sector	6.2	7½	7
GDP price deflator	5.6	6¼	5¾
Private consumption deflator	5.1	6	5½
Labour productivity	2.1	2	2
Total employment	2.9	2½	2¼
Unemployment rate	(19.5)	(18¼)	(17)
General government net borrowing (per cent of GDP)	(3.2)	(2.9)	(2.8)
Current external balance in US$	(−3.6)	(−8.1)	(−11.1)
(per cent of GDP)	(−1.1)	(−2.1)	(−2.7)

1. Based on preliminary official estimates.
2. Contribution to growth of GDP.
Source : OECD Secretariat estimates.

The additional pension-related payments and unemployment benefits announced recently will also strengthen household incomes. Yet, given fiscal drag, the growth of real household income is projected to moderate to some 4½ per cent in 1989. Subject to two opposing influences, the savings rate is projected to remain unchanged at 8¾ per cent of disposable income, slightly below the average of the previous ten years. Increasing consumer confidence based on the generalised belief that the period of recessionary tendencies has definitely ended, tends to increase the marginal propensity to consume. On the other hand, following sharp increases in personal indebtedness[30], the recent rise in interest rates should discourage consumer borrowing. This is likely to entail a marked slowdown in demand for consumer durables.

Government consumption is also projected to decelerate. All in all, a closer alignment of total domestic demand with the rate of growth of potential output is likely before the end of this year. As a result, import growth should slow down. The projected pick-up of inflation in other OECD countries and assumed absence of further upward pressure on the peseta should reinforce this tendency. As noted above, the cumulative effects on exports from the deterioration in cost and price competitiveness can be expected to be more than offset by further EC trade-creation effects and increasing export capacity. On these projections, a further reduction of the negative contribution of the real foreign balance to GDP growth would seem most likely.

The projected GDP growth of about 4¾ per cent in 1989 is considerably above the OECD average and close to Spain's potential growth. Employment should, therefore, again rise rapidly albeit slightly less than in the preceding two years, with non-agricultural employment projected to increase by 3½ per cent in the private sector and 4 per cent in general government. On this basis, the rate of unemployment may drop to around 17½ per cent by the end of 1989, along with further progress in bringing down the high rates of youth and long-duration unemployment[31].

The slower rate of decline in the trade balance in real terms is likely to be offset by less favourable terms-of-trade developments. The invisible balance may, however, show a further improvement, mainly on account of increasing transfers. In total, the current external deficit might reach close to $8 billion in 1989 or over 2 per cent of GDP. However, with foreign direct investments likely to continue on a large scale, the basic balance of payments may be broadly balanced. On the other hand, the February measures should curb the growth of financial credit and other short-term capital inflows.

In line with the official medium-term fiscal plan, some tightening of public finance is expected in 1990. This, combined with a continuing restrictive monetary policy stance, points to some further slowdown in output growth, accompanied by some easing of inflation pressure. Though less steep than in the previous few years, the upward trend of employment is likely to be maintained, reducing, according to present projections, the rate of unemployment to about 16 per cent by the end of 1990. Slower growth of domestic demand should lead to a further slowdown in import volumes and also permit resources to be shifted to the export sectors. Accordingly, the increase in the current external deficit is projected to slow down markedly.

The above projections are based on the assumption that industrial relations will become less strained and that the recent pick-up of inflation will not give an upward twist to the price-wage spiral. Given the underlying strength of the economy, such a risk clearly exists, in particular in the event of further increases in profit margins and sharply rising self-employment income. Thus, the outlook both over the short and medium run importantly hinges on the authorities' success or failure in containing inflation pressure. Faster-than-projected nominal income growth would only temporarily lead to higher real output gains as the accompanying higher inflation and deterioration of the current external balance would negatively affect foreign investors' confidence and hence investment activity, and may prompt the authorities to take restrictive measures including further increases in real interest rates.

III. Pattern and consequences of public sector growth

During the past two decades the Spanish public sector has been among the fastest growing in the OECD area. Yet, compared with more advanced countries, notably in Europe, its size in relation to GDP is still relatively small (Diagram 8), even though this does not hold equally for all expenditure components. The strong expansion of public-sector activity has been associated with rapidly mounting pressure of taxation. Given the consequent need for tighter control on both expenditure and tax collection, a number of questions arise: first, are there areas where the provision of public and merit goods, or transfers, is lagging behind current and prospective requirements; conversely, are there areas where rather the opposite seems true? Secondly, are there taxes which have been raised above reasonable limits; conversely, are there sources of taxation which should be tapped more intensively to ensure the financing of desirable public expenditure? By comparing public sector developments in Spain with those in other OECD countries, the present chapter attempts to throw some light on these questions and seeks to provide tentative answers or at least elements of them.

Institutional set-up

The public sector consists of three main areas of decision-making: the central government, which includes the State, the Social Security System and the Autonomous Administrative Organisations; the lower levels of government, consisting of the Autonomous Regions, the so-called "Autonomias", established in 1978 (henceforth called "Regions") and the local authorities (provinces and municipalities); and thirdly the public enterprise sector. The central government and territorial entities make up the general government. The Regions have a relatively high degree of political autonomy. They have an elected parliament and a government.

The central government is largely responsible for taxation, notably income taxes, social security contributions and indirect taxes. It can also borrow in foreign

46

Diagram 8. **GENERAL GOVERNMENT EXPENDITURE**
Per cent of GDP

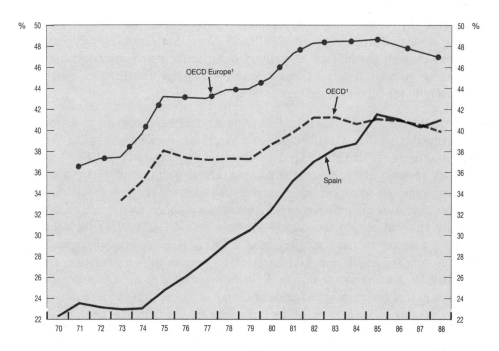

1. 1982 GNP/GDP weights and exchange rates.
Sources: OECD, *National Accounts* and OECD estimates.

currency and assumes most of the traditional spending functions of government. A substantial part of State spending consists of transfers to regional authorities, mainly to the Regions. There are three kinds of transfers: automatic transfers of tax revenues not subject to negotiations[32], transfers provided through the "Interterritorial Compensation Fund" (FCI) and central government funds for earmarked purposes. The law (LOFCA) pertaining to the annual increase of automatic transfers stipulates that if the rate of growth of taxes collected by the State for Regions is higher than the rate of growth of GDP, then the latter is taken as a ceiling so that transfers as a share of GDP remain constant. However, the law also stipulates that the total amount of automatic transfers should not increase less than State expenditure for services of a

47

similar nature to those provided by the Regions. The latter has typically been the case in the past as the State-spending ceiling has grown faster than GDP. The distribution across Regions of the tax receipts raised by the State and automatically transferred is determined by various criteria such as size of population, per capita income, area size, degree of isolation, relative poverty and "fiscal effort". State transfers provided to the Regions through the FCI are exclusively destined for new investments aimed at correcting regional disparities. Basically, FCI transfers are therefore distributed according to the infrastructural needs of each Region.

Apart from receiving State transfers, the Regions have the right to levy certain taxes (notably wealth taxes) and add surcharges on State income taxes. Without special agreement from the central government, the Regions can borrow only in domestic currency and only to the extent that debt-servicing costs (amortisation and interest payments) do not exceed 25 per cent of revenues. As regards expenditure, the Regions have wide discretionary powers, except for defence, foreign affairs, internal security and justice. For the current five-year period (1987-1991) the degree of spending autonomy varies across Regions. Only a few Regions have full responsibility for education and health care. Likewise, local authorities enjoy a large autonomy for spending, but not for revenue-raising. As to the majority of public enterprises, they do not form part of government budgets and are not therefore subject to the same direct control as other public entities. Major exceptions are the Television network and the Post Office whose budgets are voted with that of the State by the National Parliament.

Diagram 9 shows the shares of the central and lower levels of government in general government expenditure. Before the establishment of the Autonomias, the share of regional and local authorities was very small. Since 1978, it has increased continuously, primarily driven by current consumption and investment. In contrast, the dominant position of the Social Security System in the provision of public transfers has remained virtually unaffected. Regional and local authorities are now accounting for about two-thirds of fixed investment, about half of the spending for public education and a fifth of public health care. Yet, compared to Federal States, the degree of decentralisation of public spending is relatively limited. The outlook is, however, for further expansion in regional governments' expenditure shares, as some Regions are likely to demand greater responsibilities after the ending of the present five-year period in 1991.

The relative weight of public enterprises varies greatly between different sectors (Table 17). In terms of value added, the public share in 1985 exceeded 80 per cent in shipbuilding, transport and communications, but was also sizeable in the principal

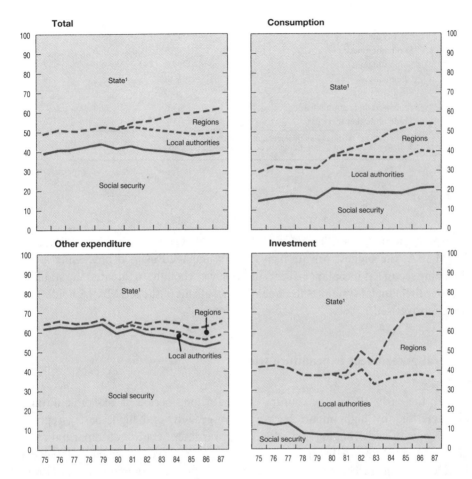

Diagram 9. **COMPOSITION OF GENERAL GOVERNMENT EXPENDITURE**

Total

Consumption

State[1]

Regions

Local authorities

Social security

Other expenditure

State[1]

Regions

Local authorities

Social security

Investment

State[1]

Regions

Local authorities

Social security

1. State is the sum of Estado and Organismos Autónomos.
Source: Instituto Nacional de Estadística.

areas of activity of the two public holdings INH and INI, i.e. energy and mining, steel and metal, and chemicals. The share of public enterprises in fixed investment generally exceeded their share in value added, reflecting relatively high capital-intensity and propensities to invest. The public sector also includes a few financial

Table 17.   **Non-financial public enterprise shares in 1985**
Percentage of sectoral total

	Value added	Fixed investment
Total non-financial public enterprises [1]	14.0	21.0
Energy and mining	45.0	65.0
Food and tobacco	7.0	26.0
Shipbuilding	95.0	94.0
Chemicals	28.0	11.3
Steel and metal	30.0	42.0
Transport and communications	83.0	97.0
Trade and other services	3.2	..

1.   Percentage relating to all non-agricultural enterprises.
Source: Annales du Centre Européen de l'Entreprise Publique, 1987.

enterprises, notably the Official Credit Institute (ICO). In 1984, the State purchased RUMASA, the biggest private firm (mainly engaged in food processing and the financing sector) as its balance-sheet situation was thought to threaten the stability of the overall financial system. Subsequently, most firms of the RUMASA holding have been reprivatised.

General government expenditure trends

In the early 1940s, the country entered a long period of economic autarchy, characterised by high import barriers, low growth, and high, partly repressed, inflation, with wide-ranging and pervasive government control of important aspects of economic activity. Although considerable resources were devoted to defence and interventions in the economy, the overall size of public spending was quite limited. Even so, the budget displayed sizeable deficits, notably during the 1950s, thus contributing to the then-prevailing situation of excess demand and relatively high inflation. In 1959 Spain became a member of the OEEC which marked the beginning of a long liberalisation process. In 1959, the "Stabilisation programme" was launched. Both the deregulation of the economy and the reduction in public deficits were key elements in what proved to be a very successful programme. Between 1960 and 1974, the Spanish economy enjoyed a period of very rapid growth, accompanied by a gentle rise of public expenditure in relation to GDP (1/4 percentage point on average per annum).

After 1974, when the economy entered a protracted period of slow growth, public spending continued to grow almost unabated at about 7 per cent per annum in real terms until 1985. As a result, the GDP share of public expenditure increased sharply. In 1985, it was twice as high as in 1967. Thereafter, real expenditure growth decelerated to about 4½ per cent per year, thus moving broadly in line with GDP growth.

The expansion of general government expenditure after 1974 was very uneven across major components. As shown in Table 18, adjusted for inflation, transfers were the most rapidly-growing component, outpacing both public investment and public consumption by significant margins. The brisk rise in transfers, apart from interest payments, essentially reflects two factors. First, the establishment of democracy was accompanied by an expansion of social welfare programmes. Secondly, given high energy-import dependency, the Spanish economy suffered more than the OECD average from the two oil shocks. As a result, payments of unemployment benefits, subsidies and capital transfers to companies rose particularly sharply. During the

Table 18.   **Decomposition of real general government expenditure growth**[1]
Annual growth rates, in per cent

	1980 / 1974	1985 / 1980	1988 / 1985	1988 / 1974
Total government expenditure	7.7	6.5	4.4	6.6
Government current consumption	6.5	3.4	5.5	5.2
of which:				
Volume effect	4.8	3.6	6.5	4.7
Relative price effect	1.7	−0.2	−1.0	0.4
Government transfers	10.3	7.3	2.9	7.6
of which:				
Volume effect	10.2	6.7	4.0	7.6
Relative price effect	0.1	0.6	−1.0	0.0
Government fixed investment	−3.3	16.5	8.6	6.0
of which:				
Volume effect	−3.1	16.9	5.2	5.5
Relative price effect	−0.2	−0.3	3.2	0.5

1.   The growth rates for the total and each component are calculated on the basis of expenditure deflated by the GDP price index. The growth rates for the three principal components are decomposed in a volume effect proper, and a relative price effect. The volume effect for a given spending component is the growth rate in nominal expenditure deflated by its own-price (the own-price of current consumption and investment are the corresponding national accounts deflators, and the consumer price deflator is used as a proxy for the own-price of transfers). The relative price effect represents the growth rate in the ratio of the own-price to the GDP deflator.
Source: OECD *National Accounts.*

1980s, the increase in public transfers has slowed down, whereas public fixed investment, which fell during the second half of the 1970s, has subsequently constituted the most dynamic component of expenditure.

A decomposition between volume and relative price components shows that the principal factor behind public consumption growth has been its rapid increase in volume, mainly reflecting strong increases in government employment. It is interesting to note in this context that the relative price effect on current consumption expenditure (the difference between changes in the public consumption deflator and the GDP deflator) was not only weak, but has turned increasingly negative during the 1980s, probably reflecting significant wage moderation. In contrast, the deflator for general government investment after 1985 grew faster than that of GDP, implying a substantial relative price effect which might reflect a change in the composition of public investment to higher-priced capital goods.

The evolution of GDP shares of the three major public expenditure categories was uneven. As can be seen from Diagram 10, the current consumption share rose slowly but continuously from the early 1970s. In contrast, public transfers more than doubled relative to GDP between the early 1970s and 1985, stabilising thereafter at about a quarter of GDP. Social Security outlays contributed most to the increase (see Annex II, Table 1). The pattern of public investment was more cyclical: it fell as a proportion of GDP until 1979, and recovered markedly throughout the 1980s.

In the early 1970s, the share of general government expenditure in GDP was below OECD and OECD Europe averages by about 15 percentage points and 19 percentage points, respectively (see Diagram 8 above). The gap was particularly wide for current consumption and fixed investment, whereas the share of transfers came close to that of the OECD as a whole (Diagram 10). After two decades, the relative size of total public spending has reached the OECD average, while remaining significantly below the OECD Europe level. The share of current consumption has remained small by international standards, reflecting a still relatively low proportion of public employment in total employment and in relation to the total population. Indeed, in 1987 government employment in relation to population in Spain was about half that of OECD Europe. By contrast, the GDP share of transfer payments exceeds the OECD average and approaches the European OECD level. The share of fixed investment, following its decline during the 1970s, more than doubled within eight years, surpassing in 1988 both the shares of total OECD and that of OECD Europe. The fact that the overall GDP share absorbed and/or redistributed by the public sector is still relatively low by international comparison could reflect Spain's retarded level of economic development relative to that of most other OECD countries.

Diagram 10. **COMPARATIVE GENERAL GOVERNMENT EXPENDITURE**

Per cent of GDP

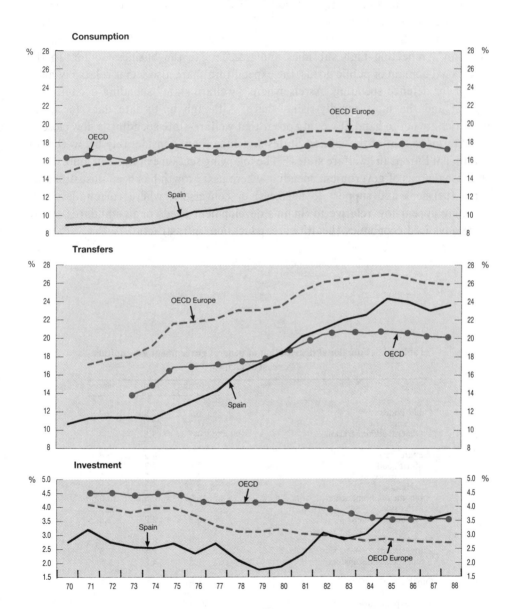

Consumption

Transfers

Investment

Note: US investment is included in consumption.
Sources: OECD, *National Accounts* and OECD estimates.

A reclassification of expenditure by government functions (Table 19) may help to throw further light on the question of where Spain may still lag behind more advanced economies and where, in comparative terms, it may already be ahead of time. In comparison with eight other OECD countries (Annex II, Table 2), Spain stands out as the country next to Italy with the highest GDP share of "mixed economy", reflecting high subsidies and transfers to the business sector. In the traditional domain of public goods, the expenditure share also seems relatively high, except for defence spending. As elsewhere, "welfare state" spending occupies the biggest and the most rapidly-rising share. Although up-to-date data for other countries are not to hand, it would appear that welfare-state spending is now close in GDP terms to that of the United States and Japan, but considerably below that of traditional European "welfare states". The following section examines in more detail functional areas of government spending where past growth has been unsustainably rapid (pensions and support to business) or conversely, where current levels of spending appear low relative to Spain's development needs or to standards set by more advanced economies (health care, education, infrastructure).

Table 19.   **Functional distribution of general government expenditure**
Per cent of GDP

	1973	1980	1986
Public goods	6.2	7.8	9.7
Defence	1.7	2.0	2.3
General administration	4.5	5.8	7.4
Welfare state	11.6	18.2	20.4
Merit goods	5.6	7.7	7.2
Education	2.3	3.7	3.5
Health	2.7	3.2	3.2
Income maintenance	6.0	10.5	13.2
Pensions	3.7	7.0	8.7
Unemployment	0.2	2.2	2.9
Mixed economy	4.0	6.1	7.8
Investment	2.2	1.4	2.3
Subsidies and transfers	1.8	4.7	5.5
Other	1.6	0.8	3.2
Total expenditure	23.4	32.9	41.1

Source: Julio Alcaide Inchausti, FIES, *Papeles de Economía,* No. 37, 1988.

Determinants and control of government expenditure

Pension benefits

Analysis and international comparison of institutional factors help explain the rapid increase in pension expenditure. The Spanish State pension system is based on the insurance principle, covering only contributors to social security. Old-age retired people, invalids and "survivors" are the three broad categories of pensioners. Over the past 15 years or so, the system has become somewhat less generous. A new Law in 1985 has changed the qualifying conditions and the income basis relevant for the calculation of future pension benefits. For most wage-earners the income basis is significantly lower than the actual wage. Between 1974 and 1985 old-age pensions were received as from the age of 65 after a minimum contribution of ten years. Earnings of the two best years (over the last seven working years) served as a basis for the calculation of the pension benefit. For pensioners with 35 or more years of contributions the latter could amount to up to 100 per cent of the income basis. After 1985, the minimum contribution period was extended to 15 years. Also the last eight best years are now taken as a reference for the calculation of the pension benefit. Another important change concerns the inflation adjustment, with benefits now being linked to official inflation targets rather than actual inflation outcomes. As regards invalidity pensions, the qualifying conditions are based on the loss of normal earning capacity, with benefits depending upon the degree of invalidity. Invalidity pension benefits range from 50 to 100 per cent of earnings. Compared with most other OECD countries the public pensions system appears to be fairly generous, notably with respect to the reference period for the calculation of the benefits. In many OECD countries, pension benefits depend on whole career earnings.

In the mid-1980s, old-age pensions accounted for 57 per cent of total pensions, compared with 65 per cent on OECD average, whereas the share of invalidity pensions was at 30 per cent well above the OECD average. Real pension expenditure growth, amounting to 10 per cent per annum during the ten-year period to 1984, can be attributed to two factors: the rise in the number of beneficiaries and changes in real benefits per beneficiary. For pensions as a whole, both factors contributed more to the rise in pension payments than on average in the OECD area. For old-age pensions, the number of beneficiaries has grown moderately faster than the old-age population as the coverage was slightly extended. At the same time, real benefits per beneficiary have grown considerably faster than average earnings, notably for those who had retired before 1974 and whose real pension value had been eroded by inflation. For invalidity and survivors' pensions, both components have shown substantial increase.

In particular, the number of invalidity beneficiaries rose at an annual rate of some 8½ per cent, about three times as much as the number of old-age pension receivers and twice as much as on OECD average. There is evidence that criteria and controls on invalidity pensions were rather lax and there is also collusion between employers and employees to abuse the system[33]. The changes in the calculation base for pension benefits and inflation-adjustment since 1985, as well as stricter application of the eligibility rules for invalidity benefits, have led to a marked slowdown in pension growth. As a result, the ratio of pension payments to GDP has stopped rising.

Support to the business sector

Another area where general government expenditure has experienced particularly rapid growth concerns support to business by way of subsidies and capital transfers. Injections of "cheap" financing capital and debt reliefs have also been used as a means of support.

Since the 1975 economic crisis financial support to industry (including funds made available under the Industrial Reconversion Programme since the early 1980s) has grown briskly. Total subsidies and transfers for economic intervention rose from nearly 2 per cent of GDP before the first oil crisis to over 5 per cent of GDP in the mid-1980s. The recent economic recovery and the resulting surge in profits was reflected in a modest decline of these types of expenditure to some 4 per cent of GDP in 1987. This is still considerably higher than in most other OECD countries. Public enterprises are the main receivers of these transfers. RENFE (the national railway company), the INI group and the General Post Office received some one-third of

Table 20. **Financial support to public enterprises**
Pesetas billion

	1977	1978	1979	1980	1981	1982	1983	1984	1985	1986	1987
Variations of net credits of the State	147.1	151.2	209.3	282.9	363.5	464.9	627.2	938.0	647.0	156.4	235.2
(Per cent of GDP)	(1.6)	(1.3)	(1.6)	(1.9)	(2.1)	(2.4)	(2.8)	(3.7)	(2.3)	(0.5)	(0.7)
of which:											
ICO	146.8	150.1	159.8	174.6	229.4	259.8	282.9	263.6	165.6	39.2	31.5
INI	..	..	..	..	..	116.0	79.4	−8.4	287.9	44.1	−76.5

Source: *Actuación económica y financiera de las Administraciones Públicas,* Ministerio de Economía, Madrid 1988.

subsidies and more than one-half of capital transfers paid by the Government in 1987.

In addition, the Government indirectly subsidises firms by providing capital finance on more favourable terms than the free market. Admittedly, part of these capital injections is used to increase the capital base of companies. Financial investments by the central government were quite sizeable in the first half of the 1980s – 2½ per cent of GDP – before falling to some ¾ per cent of GDP in more recent years (Table 20). The ICO and the INI were the main recipients. ICO mainly received capital injections, and the State also paid the debt of RUMASA, entailing a substantial rise in State debt.

Health care

The basic institutional framework for public health has been substantially altered by the 1986 law on health. Before 1986, only contributors to the financing of Social Security were covered. Others could use health facilities of benevolent institutions, and public services only on a case-by-case basis. Under the new regime, in principle, coverage is extended to the whole population so as to establish a National Health System more in agreement with the spirit of the 1978 Constitution. The legislator recognised, however, that important delays were bound to occur before the new rules could be fully implemented.

The organisation of health care has also been modified. Under the old regime, public health care was provided by a variety of central and junior government institutions. The new law aimed at unifying the system by according the role of co-ordinator and regulator to the central government and the administration of health care services to the Autonomous Regions. At present, national health care is provided by the social security health services (INSALUD), institutions of two ministries (Health and Defence), the Autonomous Regions[34], the local authorities and special central government organisations.

The financing of public health care provided by INSALUD is based both on social security contributions and State transfers. Prior to 1986, transfers were given to the Social Security without special earmarking so that these funds could be used for pensions as well as for health care. Since 1986, specific transfers have been provided for health care only. In 1989, health care is planned to be mainly financed through State transfers, with only one-quarter left to be covered by social security contributions. As regards the use of health-care services, changes have been less far-reaching. Public primary assistance is free and is provided by medical doctors who are salaried employees since 1988, with only part of their total remuneration being determined by the number of patients. A principal doctor is designated to each entitled person and the possibilities for change and choice of doctors are quite limited. Similarly, public hospital assistance is also free and is provided by salaried doctors, who also receive bonuses. The 1986 Law hardly changed this basic framework; it regrouped doctors and specialists for primary assistance within "teams for primary assistance". Besides the public health service net, there are also private doctors and hospitals part of whose services are provided on a contract basis to patients of the National Health System.

In some measure, institutional factors explain the relatively modest growth and level of public health spending. Efforts of the Social Security system to provide the necessary resources for the rapid expansion of pension benefits have undoubtedly had a negative effect on State transfers to health care services. Moreover, the lack of competition among doctors (whose remuneration is largely independent of the degree of satisfaction of patients) has probably been mirrored in relatively weak health spending growth. On the other hand, the improved coverage since the mid-1970s was bound to exert upward pressure on health expenditure. Table 21 illustrates the effects of increased coverage by decomposing real health spending among the relative price effect, the demographic effect, coverage effect and the real benefit effect. The price effect appears to be fairly weak, as the price of health services grew fairly closely in line with the GDP deflator. Real benefits have been the key factor behind the rise in the volume of health expenditure, as in most other OECD countries. Increased coverage has also contributed importantly, significantly more than in the OECD area as a whole.

During the last two years, the share of public health expenditure in GDP is officially estimated to have risen by almost ½ percentage point, implying a

Table 21. **Decomposition of health expenditure growth**
1974-1984, yearly growth rates, in per cent

| | Nominal expenditure | GDP deflator | Health prices | Relative prices | Real expenditure | *Of which :* | | |
						Demographic effect	Coverage	Real benefits
Spain	21.8	12.1	13.0	0.8	7.7	1.0	2.6	4.1
OECD	15.5	8.4	9.1	0.6	5.9	0.8	0.9	4.2

Source : OECD, Financing and delivering health care, Paris 1987.

substantial acceleration in real terms. The likely increase in coverage by virtue of the 1986 law might explain this acceleration. There was, and probably still is a widespread notion that public health care services are insufficient, as the supply of health has not kept pace with the rapid increase in demand, mirrored in relatively long waiting lists for the use of certain services, notably hospitals, and increasing recourse to private health care services[35].

Table 22. **Health : input and output indicators**

	In-patient care beds per 1 000 capita		Doctors per 1 000 capita		Consultations per capita		Infant mortality rates per 1 000 live births	Life expectancy in years
	1970	1978[1]	1970	1981[1]	1970	1981[1]	1985[1]	1979[1]
Spain	4.7	5.4	1.3	2.6	2.6	4.7	10.5	71.8
OECD	9.5	9.3	1.2	1.9	..	6.1	10.8	71.7

1. The year of reference for the OECD average is 1982.
Source : Ministry of Health and Consumption and OECD, *Financing and delivering health care,* Paris 1987.

International comparisons of some health inputs and output indicators are shown in Table 22. Spain has a very low bed *per capita* ratio. On the other hand, the number of doctors is relatively high, pointing to low productivity. Otherwise, the overall efficiency of the system seems fairly satisfactory, at least if judged by infant mortality and life expectancy. A major problem therefore seems to be the rather weak productivity of the primary health sector, with negative spillover effects to hospitals.

Education and training

Public education is virtually free at all levels with fees to cover parts of costs existing only at the university level. Schooling is compulsory between six and fourteen years. For this period a common programme of education exists (EGB). After the EGB subsequent training is provided at either professional schools or general schools. Successful completion of general schooling opens the way to university, whereas professional schooling is intended to help in finding a skilled job.

As can be seen from Table 23, the number of pre-university pupils has grown fairly rapidly since the middle of the 1970s. Particularly strong was the increase in the number of pupils in professional schools, which more than doubled during the ten years to 1985. The increase in the number of students at university was even stronger. Overall, the coverage of education has been considerably extended. Between 1975 and 1985, the enrolment rate for 15-year-olds increased by two-thirds. The number of students in higher education as a share of total population rose by nearly one-half. The number of teachers has outpaced the upward trend in schooling, so that the relatively high pupils-to-teacher ratio has decreased somewhat. In spite of considerable progress in enrolment rates, they are still among the lowest in the OECD area. However, the share of students in total population comes close to the OECD average.

The still-low coverage, combined with relatively high pupil/teacher ratios in secondary education suggest that the supply of education is not totally satisfactory. There are also signs of a growing mismatch between demand and supply of labour. The relationship between the rate of unemployment and the vacancy ratio has been shifted upwards, i.e. a given level of unemployment is now associated with more unfilled vacancies than in earlier years. This reflects the fact that despite much higher

Table 23. **Education : input and output indicators**

	1975	1985
Pre-university education		
Number of pupils (thousands)	7 517	8 696
of which :		
Public	4 340	5 593
Pre-primary	920	1 127
Compulsory	5 473	5 594
Professional post-compulsory	305	737
General post-compulsory	818	1 238
Number of teachers in public schools (thousands)	156	271
Ratio of 15-year-old pupils to population of that age	46.0	76.3
Average number of pupils per teacher in public schools	28	21
Higher education		
Students (thousands)	557	822
Number of students per 1 000 inhabitants	15.1	21.3

Source : *Proyecto para la reforma de la enseñanza,* Ministerio de Educación, Madrid 1987 and OECD, *L'enseignement dans les pays de l'OCDE,* Paris 1988.

unemployment, delays in filling a vacancy have tended to become longer. A survey by the Ministry of Labour has provided evidence that professional schools are not providing the qualifications and skills required by enterprises[36]. Ongoing educational reforms, including the introduction of Professional Training Programmes (F.I.P), are expected to improve the quality of labour supply, particularly in sectors with a skilled labour shortage.

Infrastructure

After the first oil shock, investment in infrastructure declined in real terms – a tendency which was reversed only after 1982. In particular, low investment in the transport network meant that it was unable to cope with strong demand growth, leading to a deterioration in transport conditions. Between 1975 and 1984, cumulative fixed investment per tonne-km and passenger-km for road transport was more than two-thirds below the OECD Europe average. In 1984 the ratio of the road network was 4 kilometres per 1 000 inhabitants, compared with 11 for OECD Europe. Allowing for the much lower population density in Spain the difference is even more striking. The situation in rail transportation is not much better. In fact, Spain is one of the very few countries in OECD Europe where passengers and freight by rail declined in the decade to the mid-1980s. Despite the recent pick-up in investment, transport infrastructure and equipment is still inadequate and risks becoming a serious impediment to sustained growth.

Prospective developments

When submitting the 1989 Budget proposals to Parliament the Government also presented a medium-term macroeconomic scenario and complementary fiscal projections covering the period up to 1992 (Table 24). Assuming real GDP and inflation to slow down to annual rates of growth of 4 per cent and 3 per cent respectively, the ratio of government expenditure to GDP is projected to continue to rise, though significantly less than in the past (Annex II Table 4). The principal expenditure items making for a slowdown of growth are subsidies and transfers to private and especially to public enterprises, and interest payments. The profitability of public enterprises is expected to improve and the burden of rising interest payments should ease with shrinking budget deficits and declining inflation, notwithstanding the fact that it is planned to finance a growing proportion of deficit spending at market rates.

Table 24. **Macroeconomic and fiscal scenario**

	1988	1989	1992
Macroeconomic projections			
Real GDP growth	5.0	4.0	4.0[1]
GDP deflator growth	5.7	4.0	3.0[1]
Unemployment rate	19.5	19.2	16.8
	Per cent of GDP		
Fiscal projections (Central Administrations)[2]			
Expenditure	34.6	35.0	36.0
Receipts	31.8	32.3	36.1
PSBR	3.3	3.6	0.0
Memorandum item:			
State debt/GDP ratio	37.5	38.9	34.7

1. Average annual rate 1990 to 1992.
2. Including social security system.
Source: Ministry of Finance, *Escenario macroeconómico y presuprestario,* Madrid 1988.

All other major expenditure items are projected to rise faster than nominal GDP, notably outlays on pensions, education, health care and infrastructure investment. A key assumption underlying the pension outlook is a steady increase in average old-age pension benefits so as to match the minimum wage level by 1990. On education, both the central and regional governments are expected to increase their expenditure shares. One principal aim of the Government is to raise compulsory school attendance from 14 to 16 years. Claims on resources arising from public health care are also expected to rise in relation to GDP, but the forces pushing up the share may have been underrated[37]. On infrastructure investment, the official projections incorporate a number of ambitious programmes which raise the expenditure share in GDP to 1.9 per cent by 1992, up from 0.9 per cent in 1987. The road programme alone, which includes the construction of 1 700 kilometres of motorway, amounts to the equivalent of 2.7 per cent of 1988 GDP. The railway modernisation, including the narrowing of the gauge to European standards and the introduction of high-speed trains, is expected to cost around 1 per cent of 1988 GDP, but will be spread beyond 1992.

Control and management of public expenditure

The rapid increase in government expenditure over the last 15 years has created a strong momentum of its own, with all spending departments tending to claim substantial additional resources every year. As in other OECD countries, the development of mechanisms for assessing priorities and for effectively monitoring expenditure trends has not kept pace with the rapid expansion of government activities. With the aim of increasing efficiency and improving control mechanisms, significant changes in budgetary procedures have been made in the last few years. "Committees for Functional Outlays" have been established consisting of representatives of different government departments. These fix priorities and growth profiles of outlays by function and type, which are incorporated in the four-year plans (see above: "macroeconomic scenario and fiscal projections"). The new framework of programme budgeting also helps to improve the design of annual budgets. However, there are still some institutional features of budgetary procedures which negatively affect the proper assessment of spending needs.

Since 1975, unused appropriations represented on average some 8 per cent of total credits (Diagram 11, Panel A). This suggests that some initial credits are set at relatively high levels. On the other hand, initial expenditure plans seem to be incomplete as government departments tend to ask for supplementary credit lines to be accommodated by extraordinary budgets voted in Parliament. These extra claims are frequently met, especially when revenues increase faster than budgeted and thus ensure the accomplishment of deficit-reduction objectives. As a result, the restraining effect of automatic stabilisers is weakened. There are several ways, including special cash facilities, for modifying initial budgets. In some cases, unused appropriations can be carried forward to the following year. As shown in Diagram 11, Panel B, carried-forward expenditures averaged some 6 per cent of initial budget appropriations in the three years to 1987. As a consequence, voted initial budgets may not constitute a very effective constraint to expenditure. All in all, actual expenditure has always exceeded the initial budget estimate by a wide margin, while remaining well within total credit lines.

In addition to the need to strengthen control over central government departments, and to apply stricter criteria for social expenditure and welfare entitlements, tighter control of regional expenditure would seem to be required. As already noted, regional governments, given their still relatively low debt levels, can finance rapid increases in expenditure by borrowing. Moreover, not feeling responsible to their electorate for most of tax payments, there may be a greater tendency for them to yield to persistently strong demand for more and better services. As elsewhere, there is need to strengthen the power of budget authorities *vis-à-vis* spending agencies and in order to prevent excessive overruns, ceilings on both the deficit and expenditure may have to be imposed. Cost-benefit analysis has been applied so far in a few cases only, but results have been encouraging[38].

Diagram 11. **IMPLEMENTATION OF STATE EXPENDITURE BUDGET**

Panel A
(Per cent of initial budget)

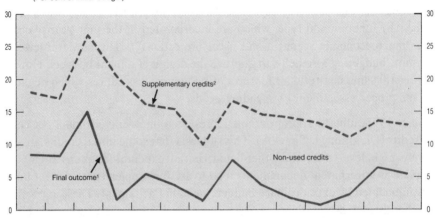

Supplementary credits[2]

Non-used credits

Final outcome[1]

Panel B
(Per cent of initial budget)

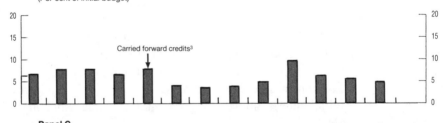

Carried forward credits[3]

Panel C

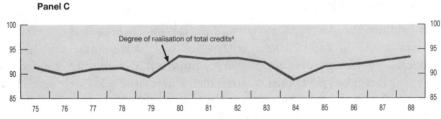

Degree of realisation of total credits[4]

1. Percentage difference between effective expenditure and initial budget appropriations.
2. Including cash facilities.
3. Credits from current budget appropriations to be spent in following years.
4. Credit commitments as a per cent of total appropriations voted in current year (initial credits plus supplementary credits).
Source: Ministerio de Economía y Hacienda.

Government revenues and tax distortions

Faced, on the one hand, with strong political and social pressure for expenditure increases, and on the other with weak economic growth between 1975 and 1985, the major concern of the Government has been to keep the rise in tax receipts broadly in line with the sharp increase in expenditure. In 1977 a comprehensive tax reform was undertaken, its principal aims being to provide Spain with a modern system of income taxation and to raise taxes, mainly on higher incomes, while at the same time introducing tax reliefs to encourage job-creation and investment. The measures included the introduction of a net wealth tax, temporarily higher taxes on above-average incomes, an extraordinary tax on corporate profits and a rise in consumption taxes for certain "luxury" goods. Tax reliefs were granted to enterprises that created jobs or invested in productive assets. In 1986, a value-added tax system was introduced. It replaced a rather complex and incomplete set of gross turnover taxes which, apart from distorting relative prices, had yielded fairly low receipts. With a view to bolstering government revenue further, the Government has also refrained from fully compensating tax-payers for fiscal drag.

Government revenues and fiscal pressure

As a share of GDP, total government revenues have increased almost continuously since the early 1970s (Table 25). The upward trend became steeper after 1977, reflecting the effects of the tax reform. Taxes on incomes and property have exhibited the greatest buoyancy. Social security contributions increased steeply as a proportion of GDP until the early 1980s. Thereafter, the trend was temporarily reversed as social security contribution rates were slightly reduced in 1985. Indirect taxes fell as a proportion of GDP until the end of the 1970s, but recovered markedly thereafter. Taxes on imports, which represented about 2 per cent of GDP until 1985, were cut dramatically from 1986, following Spain's accession to the EC. Overall, social security contributions have remained the main source of revenue, providing on average more than one-third of government receipts. Taxes on income and profits accounted for slightly more than a quarter of total revenue in 1987, which is almost 80 per cent more than in the early 1970s. Finally indirect taxes, which contributed a third of total receipts in the early 1970s, accounted for no more than a quarter in 1987.

The overall tax burden, defined as the share of total tax revenue in gross national income, has risen much faster in Spain over the past two decades than on average in

Table 25. **General government revenues**

Per cent of GDP

	1970	1975	1977	1980	1985	1986	1987
Total revenues	22.4	24.5	26.6	30.2	34.7	35.2	37.0
Tax on income, profits and property	3.4	4.4	4.9	6.8	8.4	8.1	10.3
of which:							
Taxes on personal income	2.0	2.8	2.9	4.9	6.5	5.4	7.0
Taxes on corporate income	1.4	1.4	1.2	1.2	1.6	1.8	2.3
Other	0.0	0.2	0.8	0.7	0.3	0.9	1.0
Social security contributions	7.8	10.3	11.8	13.2	13.2	13.0	13.0
Taxes on goods and services	7.8	6.7	6.7	6.8	9.7	10.9	10.3
of which:							
Taxes on production	5.9	4.7	4.8	5.2	7.9	9.9	9.4
Taxes on imports	1.9	2.9	2.9	1.6	1.8	1.0	0.9
Other revenues	3.4	3.1	3.2	4.4	3.4	3.2	3.4

Sources: *Actuación económica y financiera de las Administraciones Públicas,* Ministry of Finance, Madrid 1988, and OECD, *Revenue Statistics of OECD Member Countries, 1965-1987.*

other OECD countries (Table 26). Yet, excluding Turkey the tax share is still the smallest among OECD countries. This primarily reflects low revenues from personal income taxation. In terms of GDP they averaged just 6 per cent in the mid-1980s, the lowest figure for the OECD area along with France, Greece and Turkey. By contrast, the relative weight of social security contributions has always been well above the

Table 26. **Comparative burden of taxation**

Per cent of GDP

	Spain		France		Greece		Italy		Portugal		OECD	
	1975	1986	1975	1986	1975	1986	1975	1986	1975	1986	1975	1986
Total tax revenues	21.7	32.1	41.2	48.8	27.1	35.3	27.5	39.0	27.7	36.0	32.7	38.1
of which:												
Taxes on personal income	3.1	6.1	5.1	6.7	2.7	4.6	4.6	10.7	3.9	4.9	10.7	12.1
Taxes on corporate income	1.3	2.1	2.3	2.8	1.0	1.5	1.1	2.1	1.6	3.2	2.4	3.0
Social security contributions	10.3	13.0	16.6	20.8	6.7	10.7	12.3	13.9	9.3	9.1	7.7	9.3
Taxes on goods and services	6.7	10.7	14.0	14.5	14.3	16.5	7.5	9.1	11.2	16.6	10.3	11.5

Source: OECD *National Accounts.*

OECD average. In particular, employers' contributions are among the heaviest in the OECD area, following France and Sweden. Taxes on goods and services represented a relatively low share of GDP until the introduction of VAT but have since picked up sharply, both in relation to GDP and as a share of total government revenues.

In spite of a comparatively low personal income tax share in GDP, the tax burden for those who actually pay taxes seems much higher than in many other OECD countries. The apparent paradox is explained essentially by three factors. First, the share of taxable household income in GDP is comparatively small. Allowing for this, the personal income tax burden comes close to the OECD average. Secondly, tax evasion is high, but unevenly spread across different sources of income, more frequently occurring for self-employed and entrepreneurs than for dependent workers, and being particularly pervasive for capital income[39]. As a result, the fiscal burden primarily falls upon wage-earners, who are taxed at source. Recently, tax investigators discovered an insurance fund which had served since 1986 as a vehicle for tax evasion. Tentative estimates suggest that nearly Ptas. 2 trillion have been invested in such funds, i.e. about 5 per cent of GDP, of which 80 per cent could have been the result of tax evasion. The yield on these funds was in the range of 7 to 9 per cent, i.e. above the yield on Treasury notes. It also appears that most of the "black" money comes from the self-employed. Thirdly, apart from traditional tax allowances for children and married couples, there was until recently a fairly complex and "generous" system of non-standard tax expenditure. In 1987, the maximum non-standard tax expenditures, which an average (single) production worker could deduct from taxable income, reduced the personal income tax bill by about a quarter, a high figure by international standards, close to that of Luxemburg and Denmark[40].

The overall tax pressure on labour income can perhaps more appropriately be compared internationally by looking at the tax-wedge for a representative production worker. The tax-wedge represents that part of total compensation of employees which is taken by the government by way of social security contributions and taxes. It is a proxy for fiscal pressure on wage-earners to the extent that compensation of employees is market-determined, irrespective of the tax-wedge. The difference between gross earnings of an average production worker (including employers contribution to social security) and take-home pay can be taken as a measure for the average tax-wedge on the use of labour. As shown in Diagram 12, the tax-wedge in Spain amounted to 38 per cent of total compensation of a single production worker in 1987, slightly below the OECD average. Social security contributions, absorbing about 27 per cent of total compensation, were high compared with other countries, whereas personal income taxes (with a share of 11 per cent) were low. The tax-wedge

Diagram 12. **TAX-WEDGES AT THE AVERAGE PRODUCTION WORKER LEVEL**[a]

As a per cent of gross earnings

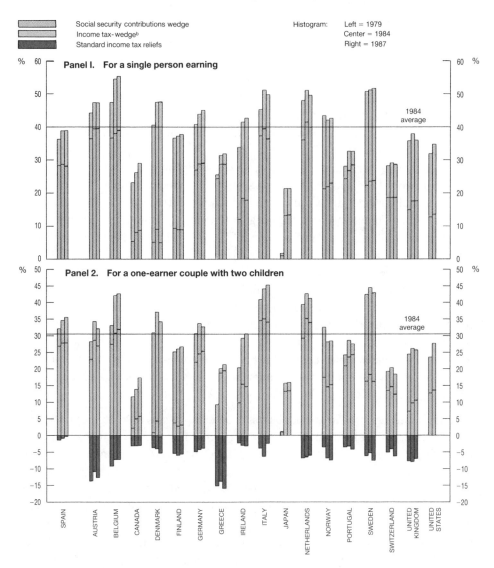

a. The tax-wedge is defined as the difference between gross earnings and earnings after direct personal income taxes (net of standard tax reliefs) and social security contributions.
Gross earnings represent the cost of labour for the employer and therefore include employer's social security contributions.
b. For a one-earner couple with two children the income tax-wedge is adjusted for standard income tax reliefs.
Source: OECD, *The tax/Benefit Position of Production Workers,* Paris 1988.

increased between 1979 and 1984 in all countries shown in Diagram 12, including Spain, tending to stabilise thereafter. In some countries it was even reduced. For one-earner couples with two children, various standard tax reliefs were allowed, with the effect of reducing the tax pressure by about 5 percentage points for the OECD average. However, standard tax reliefs hardly alleviate the tax burden in Spain, where the tax-wedge for families therefore appears to be relatively wide. However, as noted above, Spanish income-tax payers could until recently benefit more than generally elsewhere from generous special tax expenditure rules. The rising tax-wedges during the 1979 to 1984 period of pronounced wage moderation resulted in significant real after-tax wage losses which were only partially recuperated by 1987 (Table 27).

While non-standard tax reliefs helped to check the rise in average tax rates, they have not affected the upward trend of marginal tax rates (Table 28). Indeed, non-standard tax reliefs cannot reduce the tax base to which marginal tax rates apply.

Table 27. **Pre-tax and after-tax earnings of an "average production worker"**

Annual changes in real earnings in per cent

	$\dfrac{1984}{1979}$	$\dfrac{1987}{1984}$	$\dfrac{1987}{1979}$	$\dfrac{1984}{1979}$	$\dfrac{1987}{1984}$	$\dfrac{1987}{1979}$
	Single person			One-earner couple with two children		
Gross earnings	−0.5	2.1	0.4	−0.5	2.1	0.4
Take-home pay	−1.3	2.1	−0.1	−1.3	1.6	−0.2

Source: OECD, The tax/benefit position of production workers, Paris 1988.

Table 28. **Tax rates on personal income for an "average production worker"**

Per cent

	1976	1979	1983	1984	1985	1986
Marginal tax rate	15.7	17.0	19.9	20.5	33.1	33.1
Average tax rate	10.0	11.1	13.6	14.4	13.1	15.0
Memorandum item:						
Ratio of marginal tax rate to average tax rate	1.6	1.5	1.5	1.4	2.5	2.2

Source: OECD, The tax/benefit position of production workers, Paris 1988.

Estimates based on both earnings of the average production worker and on the average economy-wide wage rate suggest a doubling of average marginal tax rates between 1976 and 1986. Inflation-induced fiscal drag is probably the main factor behind this trend. Tax brackets have not been systematically and fully adjusted for inflation. Between 1977 and 1980 and in 1986 no provision was made for such adjustment of tax brackets. The effects of fiscal drag have been amplified by the strong progressivity of the tax system (Diagram 13). At times (notably in 1987) marginal tax rates were distributed in a rather peculiar way, with relatively high rates for average income brackets and lower rates for a number of higher income brackets. Such a configuration has contributed to increasing the average marginal tax rate and

Diagram 13. **MARGINAL TAX RATES ON PERSONAL INCOME**

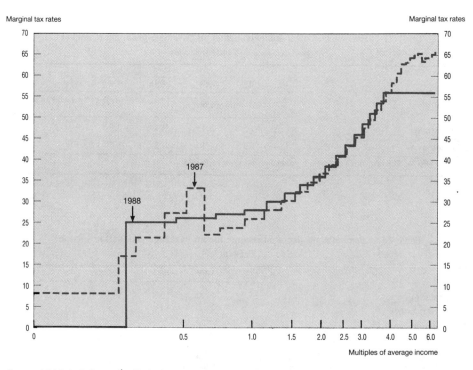

Source: Ministerio de Economía y Hacienda.

real fiscal drag. The number of tax brackets of 28 in 1979 was high by international standards, with the maximum marginal tax rate at 65.5 per cent. While the maximum rate remained broadly unchanged until 1987, the number of tax brackets was gradually increased to 34. For 1988, both the number of brackets and the maximum rate were considerably reduced, but the former is still the highest in the OECD area.

Corporate taxation is light in Spain. Corporate tax rates have remained broadly stable at about 35 per cent since the mid-1970s. Tax credits for investment and job-creation have, however, been substantially increased with the 1977 tax reform. Investment tax credits equal to 15 per cent of the cost of investment were made available (only 10 per cent when associated with a reduction in employment) and tax expenditure for job-creation amounting to Ptas. 500 000 per job was introduced. Tax credits for investment totalled 22 per cent of the corporate tax bill in 1986 and for job-creation 13 per cent.

Tax distortions

In a textbook economy where marginal costs equalise marginal gains from supply and demand decisions, a neutral tax is one which does not alter either marginal costs or marginal gains. For instance, such a tax implies that the costs of employing a worker or adding hours of overtime are fully reflected in the take-home pay. Any tax system based on the principle of marginal taxation (proportional or progressive) will lead to sub-optimal allocation of resources[41]. In reality, all modern tax systems introduce distortions into the market. The problem is how to minimise these distortions. For this the tax base should be comprehensive and defined according to economic criteria (income, expenditure, wealth, etc.); it should avoid different treatment for different kinds of consumption, investment, or saving of individuals and of production factors[42].

The choice of production factors (labour, capital) is of particular importance in an economy with high unemployment. In the event of an increase in direct taxes the final outcome on wages and employment depends crucially on both the bargaining power of the two labour market parties and on the elasticities of the demand and supply of labour. Higher taxes on wage income will affect the cost of labour if there is backward tax-shifting and employers cannot raise prices proportionally to the rise in unit costs. With the change in the political regime in 1975, unions were initially in a relatively strong bargaining position for real pay increases. However, in the wake of deteriorating labour-market conditions, the power of trade unions weakened. As regards labour demand elasticity, there is empirical evidence that the demand for labour in Spain is rather sensitive to changes in real and relative labour costs (Diagram 14). Thus, the relatively strong repercussion of taxes and social security contributions on labour costs until the end of the 1970s might have contributed to the process of capital/labour substitution during this period. Conversely, in the 1980s the moderation in wages and its favourable impact on labour demand might be partly explained by reduced tax resistance on the part of labour. Pre-tax wage moderation in a context of rising direct taxes might also reflect some sort of fiscal illusion of wage-earners as personal income taxes rather than social security contributions were the main factor behind the rise in the tax-wedge[43].

Diagram 14. **CAPITAL/LABOUR RATIO AND RELATIVE FACTOR PRICES**
Business sector

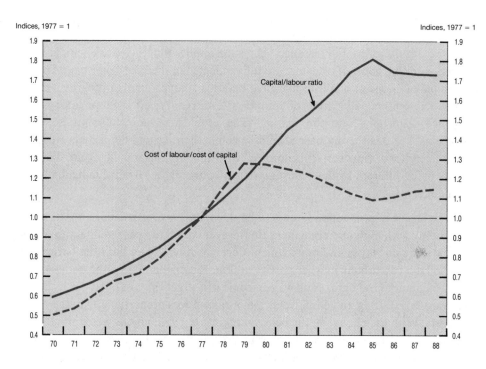

Source: OECD estimates.

The impact of widening tax-wedges on labour supply is less clear. In theory the effect of rising marginal rates on labour participation is uncertain. On the one hand, higher taxes encourage work effort to preserve income. On the other hand, by reducing the price of leisure it produces a substitution effect away from work effort. It also stimulates the black economy and occupations where taxes can be easily avoided. The rise in self-employment in non-agricultural relative to total employment by 3 percentage points between 1976 and 1986 may not be unrelated to tax consider-ations. The proposition that the uninterrupted weakening of male participation rates since the mid-1970s could reflect tax-induced discouraged work is difficult to support in the face of virtual stability of prime-age-male participation rates. However, there is some empirical evidence in support of a negative relationship between marginal tax rates and female participation rates[44].

Outlook

The macroeconomic scenario was based on the assumption that no major tax reforms would be introduced, except for adjustments in indirect taxes in the context of EC tax harmonisation. With no changes in the contribution rates, the share of social security contributions in GDP is expected to increase only marginally (by ½ percentage point). In contrast, personal income taxes are projected to rise rapidly due to the increase in real incomes, combined with an unchanged, now fully-indexed to the inflation target, structure of tax brackets and an estimated tax elasticity of 1.5. Corporate taxes are also projected to gain shares in GDP (by 0.8 percentage points), reflecting both planned measures to reduce tax expenditure for investment and job-creation in 1989 and enhanced efficiency in tax collection. Finally, capital transfers from the EC as a share of GDP are expected to double from one-third to two-thirds of a percentage point in 1992. Overall, general government receipts are projected to rise much faster than GDP, outpacing the expansion in public expenditure.

These projections do not embody the effects of three recent events. First, the recent detection of fraudulent investment funds is likely to lead to additional income for the Government, both in terms of personal income taxes and corporate taxes. Secondly, the projections neglect the effects of the reduction by half of social security contributions for new job creations with permanent contracts. This form of employment subsidy, in force in the three years to mid-1988, is applicable during the whole career of the employee. Thirdly, the Constitutional Court declared unconsti-tutional the former obligation to cumulate family income for tax purposes (see Part II). The new fiscal law, to be presented in the summer, will modify personal income taxation, but the overall tax yield should not be significantly affected. The net effect of these three factors on the Budget is likely to be marginally positive.

Government deficits and the dynamics of debt

Following the implementation of the Stabilisation Programme in 1959, the financial position of the Government improved markedly. The general government balance turned to a surplus in 1962, which lasted until 1975, except for the recession year 1971. Since the first oil-price shock, government receipts have been outpaced by the rapid increase in public expenditure, shifting the balance back into large deficits which in turn pushed up debt/GDP ratios. The objective of the macroeconomic and fiscal scenario is to bring the central governments' balance into equilibrium by 1992, which implies a fall in the debt/GDP ratio.

Government deficits

Between 1973 and 1985 the general government's financial balance deteriorated by more than 8 per cent of GDP, a much stronger worsening than in OECD Europe and the OECD area as a whole (Diagram 15). Until the end of the 1970s, the rise in the public deficit primarily reflected adverse supply and demand consequences of the first oil-price hike. But it was also boosted by stimulative discretionary measures, as the structural budget weakened during that period. From 1980 to 1985, net borrowing nearly trebled as a share of GDP, with little change of the structural deficit. The deterioration in the general government financial position was halted in 1986 owing to the cyclical upturn and consolidation policies. Although the budget consolidation process started later than in most European countries and Japan, the improvement is no less impressive. However, the persistence of high structural deficits remains a matter of concern.

The institutional composition of general government borrowing has altered importantly during the 1980s. Disregarding transfers between different sub-sectors of general government, the financial balance of the central administrations (including the Social Security System) has considerably improved: its deficit accounted for almost all general government net borrowing in 1980, whereas in 1987 its deficit was equivalent to about 2.0 per cent of GDP and that of the general government deficit 3.6 per cent. In contrast, the Regions and local authorities, whose consolidated accounts were broadly in equilibrium in the early 1980s have more

Diagram 15. **GENERAL GOVERNMENT NET BORROWING**
Per cent of GDP

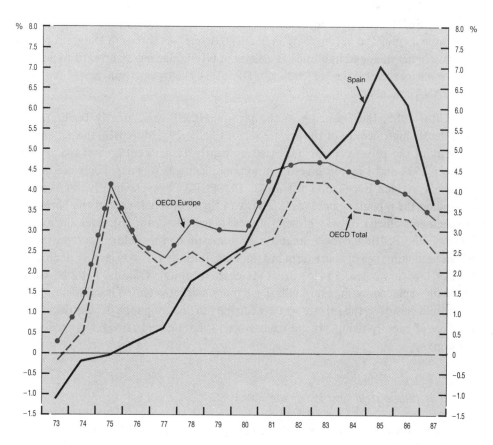

Source: OECD, *National Accounts.*

recently recorded deficits of some size. This evolution highlights the growing role of the central administration in the financing of expenditure of other levels of government.

Net borrowing as shown in the national accounts does not reflect all claims on financial resources by the general government. Additional funds are required to finance increases in financial assets. In particular, the central government has purchased shares of various companies and provided capital to ICO (see above). The total increase in general government net financial liabilities or borrowing requirements (PSBR) is equivalent to the public deficit (net borrowing of the general government) plus the net increase in financial assets. As shown in Diagram 16, the increase in net financial liabilities as a share of GDP followed an upward trend until 1984 when it exceeded the net lending/GDP ratio by a large margin, partly due to the RUMASA takeover.

Until 1985, the financing of the growing PSBR was greatly facilitated by persistently high savings of the private sector (Table 29). Moreover, the net lending capacity of the private sector increased by nearly 12 per cent as a share of GDP between 1974 and 1985, as investment in tangible assets was depressed and savings remained stable. Even so, until 1983, the PSBR was essentially financed by expanding the monetary base, as the Bank of Spain covered most of the borrowing requirements chiefly by way of zero-interest loans (Diagram 16). Ever since 1983, however, the PSBR has been financed by domestic non-monetary sources, though with a predominance of short-term instruments. Initially this was largely done in the form of Treasury notes so as to attract tax-evasion capital. Treasury notes have been gradually replaced by Treasury bills, i.e. a more market-oriented instrument. At the same time, however, the private sector's capacity to finance public deficits declined in the face of rapidly-rising private fixed asset formation and stronger propensity to consume.

The public debt and its dynamics

Rising deficits and slow growth of economic activity explain the brisk rise in the debt/GDP ratio until 1985 (Diagram 17). Thereafter, despite higher interest rates, the rise in the debt/GDP ratio abated, reflecting shrinking public deficits and steepening output growth. Overall, the size of public sector debt is somewhat below the OECD average in relation to GDP. The institutional composition of debt has changed only little during the 1980s. The State has remained by far the main debtor, with a share in total public liabilities of about 85 per cent. The share of the Autonomous Regions has increased to about 3 per cent in 1986, whereas that of the Social Security System and of local authorities has decreased.

Reflecting the move towards more market-oriented deficit-financing, the composition of State debt has been substantially modified since the late 1970s. Between 1980 and 1987, the share of debt vis-à-vis the Bank of Spain was reduced by

Diagram 16. **THE FINANCING OF THE PUBLIC SECTOR
BORROWING REQUIREMENTS**[1]
Per cent of GDP

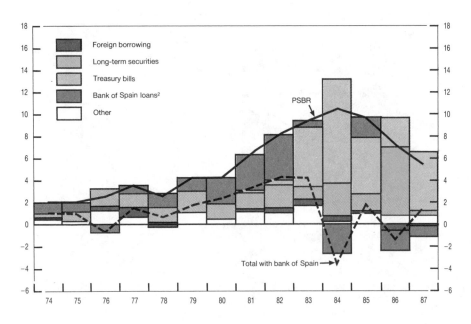

1. Measured by the increase in gross liabilities of the general government.
2. Zero-interest loans.
Source: Bank of Spain, Informe Annual, 1988.

Table 29. **Sectoral saving and net lending capacity**
Per cent of GDP

	1974	1980	1982	1983	1984	1985	1986	1987
Private sector								
Saving[1]	24.7	21.7	21.3	20.5	22.8	23.7	24.0	22.0
Net lending capacity	−3.1	0.2	3.1	3.3	6.9	8.6	7.8	3.9
General government sector								
Saving[1]	2.1	−0.8	−2.5	−2.0	−2.5	−3.3	−2.4	−0.1
Net lending capacity	−0.5	−2.6	−5.6	−4.8	−5.5	−7.0	−6.1	−3.6

1. After capital transfers.
Source: OECD *National Accounts* and OECD estimates.

Diagram 17. **GROSS GENERAL GOVERNMENT DEBT**[1]
Per cent of GDP

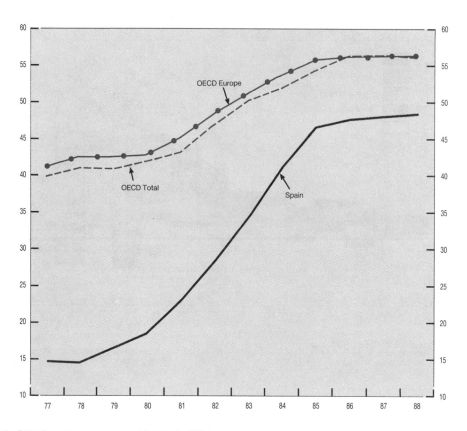

1. Ratio of average gross government liabilities to GDP.
Sources: Bank of Spain, Informe Annual, 1988 and OECD estimates.

three-quarters, to 7 per cent. Also, the debt financed by financial institutions by way of compulsory investments in low-yield securities (i.e. Treasury notes, pre-1977 long-term bonds and the RUMASA debt) accounted in 1987 for less than a quarter of total debt, compared to slightly over one-half in the late 1970s. Finally, the increased recourse to short-term instruments for the financing of the public deficit has led to a marked change in the maturity structure. After a low of one year in 1984,

Diagram 18. **INTEREST RATES AND NOMINAL GDP GROWTH**[1]

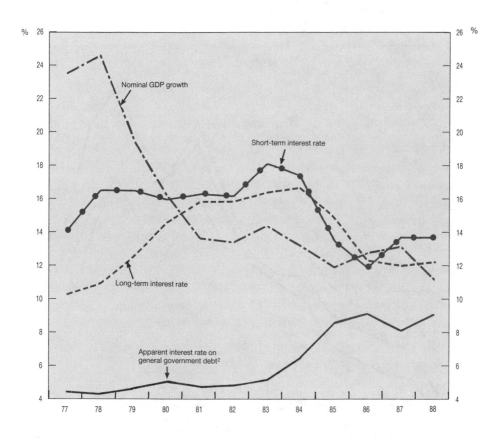

1. Two-years moving averages.
2. Interest payments in per cent of end-of-period gross government liabilities.
Sources: OECD, *National Accounts* and OECD estimates.

the average maturity lengthened to 18 months in 1987, compared with four years in the late 1970s.

The evolution in the composition of debt has translated into greater sensitivity of the apparent (or effective) interest rate to market rates (Diagram 18). Until the early 1980s, high and rising market interest rates left the low apparent cost of public debt practically unaltered[45]. Thereafter, the gap has narrowed as the apparent rate and

79

Diagram 19.   **GENERAL GOVERNMENT DEFICITS**
Per cent of GDP

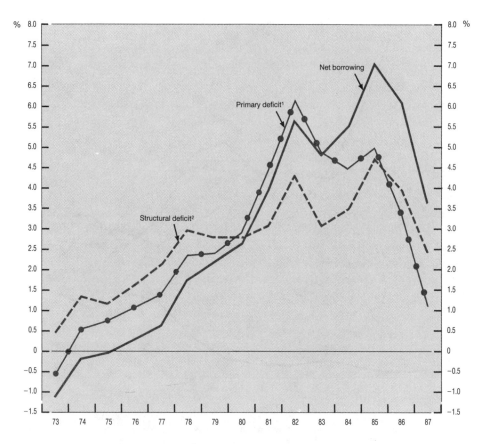

1.   Net borrowing minus net interest payments.
2.   Cyclically-adjusted balance.
Sources: OECD, *National Accounts* and OECD estimates.

the market rates followed opposite movements. Market rates experienced a steep downward trend, reflecting the on-going process of desinflation, whereas the apparent interest rate almost doubled from its average at the turn of the 1970s. Rising debt, and costs of holding it, explain the sharp increase in general government interest

80

payments as a share of GDP during the 1980s (Diagram 19). Rising interest payments (net of interest received), which had marginally contributed to the deterioration in the financial position of general government in the 1970s, have outweighed the reduction in the primary deficit during the 1980s. This could point to a risk of a vicious circle between the accumulation of deficits and an ever-growing public debt burden. Given that the primary accounts were broadly balanced in 1988, a necessary condition to prevent an explosion of debt is that the interest rate on debt does not exceed the rate of growth of nominal GDP.

The outlook for public debt very much depends on the projections for interest rates and output growth. As in most OECD countries, interest rates exceed income growth and are likely to do so in the near future. Therefore, at stable debt/GDP ratios, interest payments can be expected to rise as a share of GDP. But the debt/GDP ratio would not increase if the primary balance is turned into a surplus sufficiently large to offset the adverse impact of rising interest payments. On the hypothesis that market interest rates continue to exceed nominal GDP growth by 2.5 percentage points (which is the observed differential for 1988), the objective of stabilising the debt/GDP ratio at its 1988 level of about 45 per cent would call for a primary surplus of no less than 1.1 per cent of GDP. Given that the primary balance is not in large surplus and is likely to remain so on announced policies, the stabilisation of the debt/GDP ratio would necessitate a lower interest rate than nominal GDP growth and/or additional restraint on primary expenditure, and/or supplementary tax receipts[46].

IV. Conclusions

Since the mid-1980s the Spanish economy has exhibited remarkable strength and dynamism. Led by brisk fixed investment, real GDP expanded by more than 14 per cent over the three years to 1988, raising the level of total employment by some 8 per cent and bringing the excessively high rate of unemployment down by 3 percentage points to 18½ per cent at the end of 1988. The upswing has been accompanied by a marked increase in the domestic savings rate and a gradual reduction of the positive inflation differential *vis-à-vis* the OECD Europe average, but this has not prevented the current external balance from moving into growing deficit. However, thanks to massive long-term capital inflows, the basic balance of payments has remained in comfortable surplus and the peseta under upward pressure.

The vigour of the recovery can in part be explained by the depth of the preceding recession and structural policies pursued since the beginning of the 1980s aimed at enhancing flexibility in goods and factor markets. Moreover, the reduction of trade barriers and the huge capital inflows since Spain's entry into the EC have given a strong boost to economic activity. The Spanish economy also benefited greatly from favourable trends in world trade and oil prices. Finally, a high degree of social consensus was maintained through most of the period, minimising industrial unrest and helping to create a favourable climate for investment and job creation.

Given the momentum which economic growth has acquired both in Spain and in major trading partner countries, the prospects are for real aggregate demand to continue to grow vigorously, permitting further inroads into the still high rate of unemployment, but also implying a further rise in the current external deficit. According to latest OECD projections discussed in Part II of this Survey, the deterioration of the trade balance in volume terms should diminish from 2 per cent of GDP in 1988 to about 1 per cent in 1990, but this would still make for more than a doubling of the current deficit in terms of GDP to over 2 per cent. The size of the projected deficit should not in itself give rise to particular concern as long as high rates of return on investment attract sufficient capital from abroad and output capacity expands faster in internationally-competing industries than in domestically-oriented sectors of the economy. Indeed, this has been the case in recent years, when the investment share in GDP rose significantly and foreign capital was more than abundantly available to finance, together with rising domestic saving, the rapid expansion of Spain's output and employment-capacity. Nevertheless, prudence is required when assessing the willingness of markets to finance large and growing current external deficits over the medium term. The risk of a turnaround in market sentiment is the smaller the more successful Spain will be in sustaining a high rate of non-inflationary growth and in improving its export performance.

To maintain a favourable investment climate and external competitiveness, containment of inflation should be the prime aim of policy. Viewed against this requirement, the recent reversal of the disinflation process should be considered a matter of concern. On present trends and policies, the rise of the GDP deflator may well accelerate to more than 6 per cent in 1989 and unit labour costs in manufacturing to 4 per cent. The risk of resurging inflation relates not only to excessive domestic demand growth but also to greater union militancy in the face of persistently rising profit margins, notably in sheltered sectors. The generally favourable business situation should provide the authorities with an opportunity for speeding up the pace of deregulation and trade liberalisation as a means of keeping inflation at bay.

Since Spain's accession to the EC, the average level of tariffs has been reduced by one-half and import quotas lifted. Competition might be further enhanced as a result of new legislation on restrictive business practices. As regards capital exports, restrictions for business and individuals have been significantly relaxed since 1987. On the other hand, in order to stem the strong inflow of foreign capital, certain restrictions on borrowing from abroad have been reintroduced. The recent reorganisation of the Stock Exchange, including the abolition of the monopoly position of brokers, should enhance the efficiency of the Spanish capital market. On the fiscal side, with a view to simplifying and streamlining the tax system, the number of income tax brackets has been considerably reduced and anomalies in tax progressivity eliminated.

Measures to strengthen competitive forces further should be accompanied by a tighter overall policy stance and better balance between monetary and fiscal policy. A further rise of already-high interest rates, combined with increased upward pressure on the peseta, would certainly put downward pressure on inflation, but would bear harder on internationally-competing industries than on non-tradeable sectors. It would therefore be desirable for further policy tightening to place more emphasis on fiscal restraint. The structural deficit of the public sector, negatively affected by tax evasion, is still high and the decline in general government net borrowing from 7 per cent of GDP in 1985 to some 3 per cent in 1988 reflects more the cyclical strength of the economy than discretionary action. As on present trends government borrowing is unlikely to drop significantly relative to GDP, further efforts to strengthen public finance would seem desirable. This would also be in line with the Government medium-term objective to eliminate the deficit by 1992.

Given relatively high taxes on employment and labour income on the one hand but an internationally-low overall tax burden on the other, measures to widen the tax base and to combat tax evasion should be intensified. This will require changing tax-paying habits and tax-collecting methods. Public opinion should be made aware of the need for spreading the overall tax burden more evenly between wage and non-wage incomes. A more equitable system of taxation would induce labour to move to more productive activities and reduce incentives to moonlighting, while strengthening social cohesion and favouring continued wage moderation.

Efforts to increase tax revenue should go hand-in-hand with better control over public expenditure, all the more so as the ongoing process of decentralisation tends to stimulate public spending. As discussed in Part III, plans for improving the public education and health care systems, for extending social welfare coverage and for raising the share of infrastructure investment in total spending will entail rising claims on financial and real resources. These plans, if judged against Spain's development needs, are justifiable but make it all the more urgent to contain the growth of other expenditure items. In this respect, cost-benefit evaluations of individual programmes should be used more frequently and present rules and practices concerning the establishment and the execution of budgets need to be changed so as to keep actual spending in a given year closer in line than hitherto with initial budget appropriations.

Subsidies, transfers and capital injections into public enterprises have been reduced much less in recent years than could have been expected after three years of a booming economy. The availability and provision of budgetary funds encourage financial laxity and retard necessary structural adjustments. Thus, tighter policies *vis-à-vis* loss-making enterprises, including closures of non-viable lines of production, would help strengthen public finance. More ambitious programmes of privatisation and public asset sales could also contribute. Finally, budgetary as well as efficiency gains are likely to result from reconsidering employment subsidisation schemes from a cost-benefit point of view. Indiscriminately subsidising employment creation in a country where demand for labour is growing rapidly and labour reserves are large is not only costly in budgetary terms, but may even fail to provide incentives for the creation of viable permanent jobs. Limiting employment subsidies to new hirings with indefinite contracts does not solve the problem of subsidising jobs which would have been created anyway – in fact it tends to make such deadweight losses even bigger – nor would it seem reasonable to discriminate against more flexible types of employment contracts. On these considerations, employment subsidies are difficult to justify unless they are aimed at disadvantaged groups in the labour market. More generally, government assistance to professional training and retraining as well as financial incentives to hire long-term unemployed people would seem reasonable in the light of Spain's staggeringly high youth unemployment and the rapid process of industrial restructuring.

As the operative constraint on output is scarcity of capital rather than labour or lack of profitability, future employment growth will crucially depend on two factors: the rate of growth of the stock of productive capital and changes in capital/labour intensity. To maximise employment growth both factors can be positively influenced by nominal and real wage moderation. Real wage gains should generally not exceed underlying productivity growth with wage structures across industrial sectors, regions and skills brought into better line with supply and demand conditions in individual labour markets. This would help to improve both the quality of labour supply and employment opportunities for low-skilled labour. Meanwhile, moderate increases in nominal wages are instrumental in keeping inflation at bay and international competitiveness intact, thereby creating conditions for maintaining actual output close to its potential level.

In the present situation, characterised by the absence of social concertation, the capital constraint on output risks becoming more severely and quickly binding, for two inter-related and mutually-reinforcing reasons. First, if wage settlements significantly exceeded the cautious OECD projections discussed in Part II, the monetary policy stance would be likely to become tighter, with negative effects on the return on past investments and investment activity. Secondly, if industrial relations become increasingly strained, investors' confidence would be undermined and the net capital inflow from abroad would certainly slow down. In view of these risks, it would seem important for concertation between the authorities and the two sides of industry about the appropriate evolution of incomes to be strengthened. In the case of Spain, where more than one-fifth of total labour supply (including discouraged job-seekers) is without a job and where most social benefits are directly or indirectly linked to wage developments, the two labour-market parties willy-nilly carry responsibilities which transcend pay increases or labour costs for their respective constituencies. In these circumstances, a better-informed process – and more efficient outcomes – could be fostered by institutionalised, regular tripartite contacts and meetings, including participation of independent experts and analytical inputs of economic research institutions. Needless to say, this calls for further improvements in statistical monitoring of income and productivity developments, so as to provide a reliable basis for income negotiations and tax/transfer policies.

Summing up, economic policies and a favourable international environment have set the Spanish economy on a steep growth path. Persistently strong domestic demand pressure has, however, entailed a reversal of the disinflation process and, together with a rising peseta, has led to a further weakening of international competitiveness and the current external position. Sustaining a path of non-inflationary growth requires further budget consolidation both in central and regional administration, and better co-ordination with monetary policy. The risk of over-heating can be reduced by stepping up microeconomic reforms and by speeding up trade liberalisation and abolishing other barriers to competition, notably in the service sector. It is also important to re-establish a more favourable climate of industrial relations so as to assure wage moderation, a key condition for maintenance of foreign investors' confidence and high rates of employment-creating capital formation.

Notes and references

1. Following the recent surge in productive investment, the rate of growth of potential output is estimated to have attained 4½ per cent in 1988-89, up by about 1 percentage point since the mid-1980s. This estimate is based on capital stock calculations, using the perpetual inventory method, on underlying total factor productivity gains and on the economically usable labour force.

2. Simulation results of the INTERLINK model for Spain suggest that business and real estate foreign direct investment constituted the main exogenous source of growth since 1986 (see Annex I).

3. Rents and real estate prices are reported to have risen by about 50 per cent between 1986 and 1988.

4. Production statistics are incomplete and not wholly reliable. The growth rates in Table 2 have been based on market price values and should therefore be taken as broad estimates. As the available index of industrial production is based on 1972 production structures it has to be used with caution. It tends to under-estimate actual growth rates but can still be relied upon as an indicator for turning points or *significant* acceleration or deceleration in growth rates.

5. Agricultural employment declined by 37 per cent between 1977 and 1988, or by 1 million in eleven years. Agricultural employment in 1987 was down to 1.7 million, 15 per cent of total employment, compared with 21 per cent in Portugal, 10 per cent in Italy, and 7 per cent in France.

6. Employment in the general government sector increased by some 3¼ per cent but declined in public enterprises and firms.

7. In a nutshell, two kinds of labour market measures have been taken during the past eight years or so: first, measures aimed at making labour a more flexible and adaptable input with respect to changing economic conditions, notably by facilitating the creation of part-time and temporary jobs; secondly, measures to reduce the cost of new hirings by lowering (by half) social security contributions for net additions to the workforce with indefinite contracts, by an annual subsidy of Ptas. 400 000 (slightly below the annual minimum wage) for conversions of temporary into indefinite contracts, and by tax expenditure (worth Ptas. 500 000 in 1988) for any net addition to the average annual workforce irrespective of the type of contract. For details of these measures see OECD, *Economic Surveys of Spain.* April 1986 and January 1988.

8. By restricting tax reliefs to net creation of *permanent* jobs (as is the case for the employment subsidy), the deadweight losses accompanying any employment subsidisation schemes will be increased, while labour market flexibility will be reduced. The deadweight loss is the cost of subsidising employment-creation that would in any case have taken place.

9. The decline in tariffs *vis-à-vis* its EC partners was 15 per cent in 1988, making for a cumulative decline of 38 per cent since joining the EC. Additional reductions of quotas and other trade barriers both *vis-à-vis* EC countries and third countries have also stimulated imports.

10. In 1988 Spain's imports from the EC represented 57 per cent of total imports compared with 58 per cent (arithmetic average) of other EC countries and 59½ per cent of total intra-EC trade in total EC trade. The corresponding export shares were 66 per cent, 60 per cent and 63 per cent.

11. See OECD, *Economic Survey of Spain*, January 1988, pp.20-25.

12. Given the rise in foreign exchange reserves, this item also seems to have been considerably inflated by the large positive interest rate differential between Spanish rates and those in which official reserves are being held.

13. Since up to half or more of these direct investment flows may be associated with extra imports or may induce additional imports via income-generation, it could be argued that the current account would have remained in broad balance in 1988 had it not been for these types of capital inflows and the accompanying extra investment.

14. So far only data on State government receipts and expenditure have been published. Tax receipts and expenditure in 1988 for other levels of government are OECD estimates.

15. In 1987, tax receipts from personal incomes grew even more rapidly, since tax brackets and marginal tax rates were maintained unchanged and income tax withholding for employees was shifted from a quarterly to a monthly basis. The latter inflated tax receipts in 1987 and lowered them in 1988.

16. Underlying the budget estimates was an inflation of 4 per cent (year-on-year) compared with an outcome of 4.8 per cent. Average earnings in the economy as a whole were assumed to rise by slightly over 5 per cent, nearly 1 percentage point less than the outcome. Moreover, the unexpected decline in oil prices in world markets led to an increase in indirect tax receipts by nearly 0.2 per cent of GDP.

17. The number of tax brackets was reduced from 34 to 17 and the top marginal tax rate from 66 to 56 per cent. In addition, taxable incomes up to Ptas. 600 000 were exempted, thereby freeing almost 1 million people from paying taxes. These changes entailed a small reduction in the average tax burden.

18. Most of the EC capital transfers are given on condition that additional funds are provided by the Spanish Government for the same projects.

19. Basic rates for civil servants were raised by 4 per cent, based on the assumption that inflation would fall to 3 per cent in the twelve months to December 1988. Pay adjustments for employees in the social security area were, however, significantly higher.

20. The State increased the capital base of a number of companies under its control (notably Banco Exterior and Telefonica) by buying additional shares and providing loans to CESCE – an export insurance institution – to cover political risks for Spanish exports.

21. Treasury bills of one-year maturity, introduced in June 1987, are sold through auctions to individuals, companies and financial institutions. The Bank of Spain uses this instrument for open-market operations through repurchase agreements of three months or shorter periods. Likewise, financial institutions can place these bills with the general public through repurchase agreements. This system also applies to government bonds. Treasury notes are sold at very low interest rates – around 5½ per cent in 1988 – but as banks are not obliged to report the holders to the tax authorities, they are used as a vehicle for tax evasion.

22. The percentage increase in tax allowances is the same as the original official inflation target, which was subsequently dropped.

23. It has also been announced that the new fiscal law will abolish tax reliefs for the purchase of a second house.

24. See section on "Structural policies".

25. The cash deposit of 6.5 per cent is part of the "minimum reserve requirements" of 18 per cent of eligible liabilities. The rest – 11.5 per cent – are in the form of interest-bearing deposits with the Bank of Spain carrying interest rates considerably below market rates.

26. The unexpected drop in external demand for electrical equipment and the replacement of ITT, the major shareholder, by Alcatel motivated the extension of the reference period.

27. The trade deficit on a cash basis rose to $5.0 billion in the first three months of 1989 compared with $2.9 billion a year earlier. Over the same period the current account switched from a surplus of $400 million to a deficit of $3.3 billion.

28. Corrective pay adjustments for the overshooting of the 3 per cent inflation target for 1988 are estimated to add about 1 per cent to basic pay in 1989.

29.

Procurement bids for public works

	1988	1986	1987	1988
	Pesetas billion	Percentage change		
Total government	990	0.6	22.2	36.6
Central government	521	−11.5	51.7	28.6
Autonomous and Local governments	469	13.3	−2.0	47.0

30. Between end-1986 and end-1988 bank loans to individuals increased by over one-half, within which credit for consumer durables rose by 90 per cent. At the end of 1988, outstanding debt of households, though still low by international standards, amounted to 19 per cent of disposable income, compared with 14½ per cent in 1986.

31. Registered unemployment was down to 2.7 million in March 1989, 300 000 less than a year earlier.

32. The "historical" Regions (the Basque country and Navarra) are excluded from the system of State tax transfers as they have their own tax authority, with a small part of tax revenue transferred to the State.

89

33. The cost to employers of invalidity pensions is insignificant compared with the cost of redundancy and to employees the invalidity pension is much higher and more lasting than unemployment benefits.

34. At present four Autonomous Regions (Andalucia, Catalonia, Basque Country and Valencia) are fully responsible for the integrated public health services. In the rest of the Autonomous Regions, the INSALUD administers social security health care services, while the Regions provide selected health services (e.g. vaccinations).

35. INSALUD estimates show that between 1985 and 1988 admissions to hospitals increased by 11.6 per cent, outpatient consultations by 24.5 per cent, surgery by 22.9 per cent and the use of emergency services in hospital by 33.9 per cent.

36. There is excess demand for certain skills, notably in the construction sector and computer services.

37. The underlying trend elasticity of demand for health care with respect to income growth is – at an estimated 1.9 – relatively high. Moreover, with real incomes rising fast, the relative price effect is likely to become more pronounced than allowed for in the projections; and finally, with improved public health care, there is likely to be a shift away from privately-financed health services.

38. For examples of cost-benefit experiences in OECD countries see "The Control and Management of Government Expenditure", OECD 1987.

39. According to available studies pertaining to 1980, 25 per cent of dependent workers avoided taxation, two-thirds of self-employed did not declare income for taxation and more than three-quarters of capital revenue escaped taxation.

40. In the 1980-86 period, allowances for housing investment (a third of the value of total allowances), acquisition of financial securities (slightly less than a third) and business fixed investment (12 per cent) were the most important non-standard tax reliefs. Some of the non-standard tax reliefs have been reduced since then.

41. Only lump-sum taxes or per capita taxes satisfy such a condition. An exhaustive exposition of the welfare principles is to be found in Maurice Allais, "Traité d'économie pure", Paris 1943; see notably Chapter 4 "on the dynamics of equilibrium".

42. For a description of tax systems which are neutral with respect to these decisions, see Joseph Pechman, *Tax Reform: Theory and Practice*, Economic Perspectives, I9(1), Summer 1987.

43. To the extent that social security benefits are contribution-related and contributions are perceived by the worker as an insurance fee rather than a tax, social security contributions from employers and employees alike do not drive a wedge between labour costs and real remuneration.

44. See Garcia, J., Gonzalez, I. and Zabalza, A. *The Determinants of Labour Supply Decisions by Spanish Females*, mimeo, Madrid 1988.

45. The apparent cost of debt (or apparent interest rate) is measured by the ratio of interest payments to gross debt.

46. The official macroeconomic projections incorporate a slight fall in the debt/GDP ratio assuming interest rates to fall to levels close to nominal GDP growth and the primary balance to move into surplus.

Annex I

Simulated macroeconomic effects of foreign investment

Foreign direct investment as derived from Spanish balance of payments statistics , comprises business direct and real estate investment. It averaged just below 1 per cent of GDP during the fifteen years to 1985 and doubled to 2.0 per cent since. The OECD INTERLINK model for Spain has been used to trace out the effects of the surge in foreign investments.

Part of these investments might not have been translated into fixed investment but this can be assumed to be broadly offset by the fact that private fixed investment was also stimulated by two important capital import items for which no data exist: portfolio investment representing capital injections into foreign subsidiaries in Spain and borrowing from abroad by foreign firms to finance fixed investment.

The INTERLINK model for Spain is essentially demand driven but it also incorporates a supply block[1]. Private fixed asset formation is modelled as a function of relative factor prices (proxied by the ratio of the user cost of capital to gross compensation per employee) and expected output, which is determined by actual demand, capacity utilisation and profitability. However, the equation substantially underestimates the investment boom since 1986 and this may in a large measure be attributable to the autonomous nature of foreign capital inflow.

The simulation embodies an unchanged policy stance for both monetary and fiscal policy, in the sense that real interest rates and real fiscal expenditure are maintained constant during the simulation period. The effective exchange rate also remains unchanged in nominal terms. A simulated rise of exogenous foreign investment translates in the first instance into higher demand for capital goods and stronger activity. Higher output, in turn, leads to a marked increase in employment and through an investment acceleration type function into an even higher business investment. The fall in unemployment exerts upward pressure on nominal wage advances and hence on unit labour costs and inflation. Over time fixed asset formation gradually augments the productive capacity of the economy, thereby attenuating inflationary pressures.

Simulation results for 1986-1988 are presented in the table. The simulated effects show the responses of the main macroeconomic variables to the exogenous increase in foreign direct investment since 1986. The simulations suggest that foreign capital inflows have lent strong support to the upturn in activity "explaining" one-third of cumulated GDP growth, 30 per cent of jobs created and half of private fixed asset formation. The weak simulated price effects are mainly due to the moderate impact of unemployment on nominal wages.

Annex I Table.   **Simulated effects of foreign direct investment**

Per cent

	1986	1987	1988	$\dfrac{1988}{1985}$
	Annual growth rates			Cumulative change
Output				
Simulated effect	1.1	1.5	2.0	4.5
Observed	3.3	5.5	5.0	14.4
Private investment				
Simulated effect	6.7	7.9	9.8	24.4*
Observed	10.4	17.4	14.4	48.3
Total employment				
Simulated effect	0.3	0.8	1.4	2.5
Observed	2.2	3.1	2.9	8.4
Change in rate of inflation (GDP price deflator)				
Simulated effect	0.0	0.2	0.2	0.4
Observed	2.4	−5.0	−0.3	−2.9

Source :   OECD INTERLINK Model.

To the extent that foreign direct investments have left the peseta at a higher level than would otherwise have been the case, the price effect was less "positive" and could have been even negative. The impact of a higher peseta on real output is more ambiguous over the short to medium-run, the direction depending on the relative strength of the positive terms-of-trade effect on real domestic demand and the negative competitive effect on the real foreign balance.

Note

1. For a detailed analysis of the OECD INTERLINK model see: "The structure and simulation properties of OECD's Interlink model" by Pete Richardson, *OECD Economic Studies N° 10*, spring 1988.

Annex II

Public sector : selected tables

Annex II   Table 1.   **General government expenditure**
Yearly average, as a percentage of GDP

	Spain				OECD Europe				OECD			
	1974-76	1979-81	1984-86	1987	1974-76	1979-81	1984-86	1987	1974-76	1979-81	1984-86	1987
Current consumption	9.7	12.1	13.3	13.9	17.3	18.5	18.9	18.7	17.1	17.0	17.6	17.6
Wages and salaries	7.8	9.6	10.5	10.3	11.7	12.4	12.6	12.4	11.2	11.0	10.9	10.9
Goods and services	1.9	2.5	2.8	3.6	5.6	6.1	6.3	6.3	5.9	6.0	6.7	6.7
Transfers	12.3	18.0	23.6	22.7	20.8	23.6	26.7	26.0	16.1	18.0	20.6	20.2
Social security outlays	8.6	12.5	14.7	14.4	13.9	15.5	16.9	16.8	11.5	12.5	13.6	13.5
Subsidies and capital transfers	2.0	3.3	4.4	3.3	3.3	3.4	3.4	2.9	1.9	2.0	2.0	1.8
Interest payments	0.5	0.7	3.0	3.4	2.1	3.0	4.6	4.5	1.6	2.3	3.7	3.6
Other current transfers	1.3	1.5	1.6	1.5	1.5	1.7	1.8	1.8	1.1	1.2	1.3	1.3
Gross investment	2.5	2.0	3.5	4.0	3.9	3.1	2.8	2.8	4.4	4.1	3.6	3.6
Government expenditure (total)	24.6	32.1	40.4	40.6	42.0	45.2	48.4	47.5	37.6	39.1	41.8	41.4
Government expenditure (excluding interest payments)	24.1	31.4	37.4	37.2	39.9	42.2	43.8	43.0	36.0	36.8	38.1	37.8

Sources : OECD, National Accounts, 1974-1986, Paris 1988 and OECD, Economic Outlook, Paris, December 1988.

Annex II   Table 2.   **Functional distribution of government expenditure in 1981**

Per cent of GDP

	Spain	Austria	Denmark	France	Germany	Italy	Japan	United Kingdom	United States
Public goods	7.8	6.8	8.0	7.5	6.8	7.0	4.2	7.7	8.4
Defence	2.0	2.6	2.6	3.8	2.9	2.0	0.9	4.5	4.7
General administration	5.8	4.2	5.4	3.7	3.9	5.0	2.3	3.2	3.7
Welfare state	18.2	19.1	33.8	33.2	31.0	29.8	19.4	22.7	18.0
Merit goods	7.7	11.7	17.4	16.0	14.3	14.0	12.5	13.6	10.2
Education	3.7	5.7	8.4	5.9	5.2	6.1	4.9	5.1	5.7
Health	3.2	4.7	5.7	6.4	6.8	6.0	4.7	4.4	3.7
Income maintenance	10.5	7.4	16.4	17.2	16.7	15.8	6.9	9.1	7.8
Pensions	7.0	5.6	8.1	11.9	12.6	13.1	4.7	6.5	6.7
Unemployment	2.2	0.8	5.1	1.9	1.4	0.6	0.4	0.7	0.4
Mixed economy	6.1	3.9	5.3	3.9	4.9	7.5	6.0	3.6	3.2
Infrastructure Investment	1.4	1.8	..	1.0	2.0	2.8	3.6	1.2	0.7
Subsidies and capital transfers	4.7	2.1	..	2.9	2.9	2.7	2.3	2.5	2.5
Other	0.8	4.1	12.4	4.6	6.6	6.9	4.9	9.2	3.2
Total expenditure	32.9	33.9	59.5	49.2	49.3	51.2	34.5	43.2	32.8

Sources :   OECD, *Economic Studies,* No. 4, "The Role of the Public Sector", Tables 9 and 10, Paris 1985; FIES; Secretariat estimates.

Annex II   Table 3.   **Infrastructure equipment investment : selected statistics**

	Cumulative road investment (1975-84) per kilometre of road traffic	Total gross investment in ground transport infrastructure (as a share of GDP)	
		1975	1983
Austria	0.83	2.3	1.6
Belgium	0.57	1.9	1.3
Denmark	0.47	1.3	0.7
Finland	0.43	1.9	1.3
France	0.40	1.3	0.9
Germany	0.55	1.8	1.2
Italy	0.20	1.1	1.0
Norway	0.84	1.8	1.1
Spain	**0.21**	**1.5**	**1.0**
Sweden	0.41	1.1	0.8
Switzerland	0.78	2.2	1.7
United Kingdom	0.21	1.0	0.6
Average	0.49	1.6	1.1

Source :   ECMT, *Investment in transport infrastructure in ECMT countries,* Paris 1988.

Annex II   Table 4.   **Macroeconomic and fiscal scenario**

	1988	1989	1990	1991	1992
Macroeconomic projections					
Real GDP growth	4.7	4.0	3.5	4.0	4.4
GDP deflator growth	5.1	4.0	3.0	3.0	3.0
Unemployment rate	19.8	19.2	18.7	17.8	16.8
Central Administrations	Per cent of GDP				
Expenditure projections					
Total expenditure	34.6	35.0	35.8	35.9	35.9
of which :					
Pensions	8.3	8.7	8.7	8.8	8.9
Health	3.9	4.0	4.0	4.0	4.1
Education	1.7	1.9	1.9	2.0	2.1
Infrastructure	1.1	1.4	1.5	1.5	1.6
Subsidies and capital transfers	4.4	3.1	3.4	3.3	3.3
Interest payments	2.8	2.7	2.8	2.7	2.5
Transfers to territorial governments	4.0	4.2	4.2	4.2	4.3
Receipts projections					
Total receipts	31.8	32.3	34.0	35.0	36.1
of which :					
Personal income taxes	6.8	6.9	7.1	7.5	7.9
Corporate taxes	2.2	2.4	2.6	2.8	3.0
Social security contributions	10.7	11.1	11.1	11.2	11.3
Indirect taxes	8.9	8.9	9.3	9.6	10.0
Capital transfers from EEC	0.3	0.4	0.5	0.6	0.6
Deficit projections					
Net borrowing[1]	2.8	2.7	1.8	0.9	−0.1
Net increase in financial assets	0.5	0.9	0.2	0.2	0.1
Net increase in financial liabilities[2]	3.3	3.6	2.0	1.1	0.0

1.   Difference between total expenditure and total receipts.
2.   The net increase in financial liabilities represents the financing needs of Central Administrations and is obtained by adding
     the net borrowing to the net increase in financial assets.
Source :   Ministry of Finance, Escenario macroeconómico y presupuestario, Madrid 1988.

STATISTICAL ANNEX

Table A. **Main aggregates of national accounts**
Billion pesetas

	Current prices					1980 prices				
	1983	1984	1985	1986	1987	1983	1984	1985	1986	1987
I. Expenditure										
1. Private consumption	14 808.1	16 370.0	18 137.7	20 435.7	22 713.6	10 072.8	10 034.1	10 273.3	10 644.1	11 224.5
2. Government consumption	3 090.9	3 448.3	3 906.6	4 470.0	5 141.7	2 141.7	2 203.3	2 305.5	2 437.5	2 649.3
3. Gross fixed capital formation	4 574.6	4 708.6	5 275.6	6 124.0	7 386.1	3 191.7	3 006.8	3 131.4	3 444.2	3 947.6
a) Construction	2 876.9	2 972.8	3 274.8	3 696.9	4 318.6	2 025.4	1 920.8	1 958.5	2 085.8	2 294.4
b) Machinery and equipment	1 697.7	1 735.8	2 000.8	2 427.1	3 067.5	1 166.3	1 086.0	1 172.9	1 358.4	1 653.2
4. Changes in stocks	–104.4	4.2	–34.9	208.0	406.0	–59.1	2.8	–19.4	126.5	239.6
5. Exports of goods and services	4 725.6	5 943.5	6 518.7	6 475.9	7 023.9	3 014.4	3 367.9	3 460.4	3 505.0	3 710.7
6. less: Imports of goods and services	4 860.1	5 363.3	5 914.8	5 766.1	6 956.7	2 728.5	2 700.5	2 868.4	3 341.0	4 023.0
7. Gross domestic product at market prices	22 234.7	25 111.3	27 888.8	31 947.5	35 714.5	15 633.1	15 914.5	16 282.8	16 816.4	17 748.7
II. Output by sector										
1. Agriculture, forestry and fishing	1 370.2	1 642.7	1 744.4	1 814.5	1 941.5	1 016.6	1 104.1	1 138.4	1 034.9	1 134.2
2. Industry	6 741.3	7 669.4	8 492.8	10 321.7	11 034.4	4 599.8	4 649.7	4 747.0	5 013.5	5 277.6
3. Construction	1 631.7	1 635.6	1 806.1	2 226.6	2 860.0	1 316.6	1 235.5	1 263.2	1 338.1	1 477.5
4. Services	13 082.0	15 168.0	16 849.5	18 967.3	21 445.2	9 000.6	9 239.0	9 452.8	9 774.0	10 229.5

Source : INE, National Accounts, Madrid 1988.

Table A. Main aggregates of national accounts *(cont'd)*

Billion pesetas

	1982	1983	1984	1985	1986	1987
III. National income						
1. Compensation of employees	9 853.2	11 132.4	11 876.2	12 891.0	14 600.4	16 354.4
of which: Wages and salaries	7 554.8	8 494.5	9 100.2	9 757.5	10 998.8	..
Employers' contributions to social security	2 323.4	2 667.9	2 805.3	3 165.1	3 638.4	..
Net compensation from abroad	–24.3	–30.0	–31.3	–31.5	–36.9	..
2. Gross operating surplus	8 680.8	9 778.0	11 667.3	13 049.6	14 540.8	16 729.4
Households and private non-profit institutions	5 176.8	5 906.8	6 905.0	7 696.2	8 481.2	..
Corporate and quasi-corporate enterprises	3 398.4	3 744.6	4 614.2	5 184.6	5 865.1	..
General government	105.6	126.6	148.1	168.8	194.5	..
3. Consumption of fixed capital	2 253.7	2 637.9	3 029.6	3 349.2	3 626.5	3 943.3
4. Net national income at factor cost	16 280.3	18 272.5	20 513.9	22 591.4	25 514.7	29 140.5

Source: INE, *National Accounts*, Madrid 1988.

Table B. Income and outlay transactions of households

Billion pesetas

		1981	1982	1983	1984	1985	1986
1.	Compensation of employees	8 734.4	9 877.4	11 162.3	11 907.5	12 922.5	14 637.2
2.	Property and entrepreneurial income, net	4 376.0	5 176.8	5 906.8	6 905.0	7 696.2	8 481.2
3.	Other income from property	482.9	524.4	558.3	632.4	919.4	1 051.7
4.	Current transfers	3 076.0	3 539.3	4 105.5	4 550.2	5 200.2	5 865.0
	Of which: Social security and social assistance benefits	2 639.2	3 012.2	3 509.2	3 947.5	4 480.1	5 026.6
5.	Change in the actuarial reserves for pensions	2.2	1.5	0.0	15.3	47.0	132.0
6.	Current receipts	16 671.5	19 119.4	21 732.9	24 010.4	26 785.3	30 167.2
7.	Final consumption expenditure	11 457.9	13 143.3	14 808.1	16 370.0	18 137.7	20 435.7
8.	Direct taxes on income and property	925.9	981.5	1 313.9	1 604.0	1 822.4	1 952.1
9.	Current transfers	2 816.3	3 206.7	3 703.5	3 981.0	4 468.6	5 176.9
	Of which: Social security and social assistance contributions	2 144.4	2 457.6	2 838.7	3 057.4	3 384.8	3 855.0
10.	Current disbursements	15 200.1	17 331.5	19 825.5	21 955.0	24 428.7	27 564.7
11.	Disposable income (6-8-9)	12 929.3	14 931.2	16 715.5	18 425.4	20 494.3	23 038.2
12.	Gross saving	1 471.4	1 787.9	1 907.4	2 055.4	2 356.7	2 602.5
13.	Saving rate, per cent (12/11)	11.4	12.0	11.4	11.2	11.5	11.3

Source: INE, *National Accounts,* Madrid 1988.

Table C. **Public sector accounts**

Billion pesetas

	1983	1984	1985	1986	1987
		1. General government			
Current account					
Receipts					
Gross operating surplus	126.6	148.1	168.8	184.1	198.5
Property income receivable	307.1	251.7	324.7	356.5	279.7
Indirect taxes	1 900.1	2 271.4	2 686.9	3 565.5	3 892.5
Direct taxes on income and wealth	1 748.1	2 085.6	2 378.4	2 681.0	3 731.1
Actual social contributions	2 787.3	3 011.0	3 354.2	3 794.1	4 273.0
Imputed social contributions	267.2	271.2	319.9	346.7	363.2
Miscellaneous current transfers	555.4	606.6	733.0	907.9	1 045.5
Total	7 565.2	8 497.5	9 797.1	11 651.7	13 585.0
Disbursements					
Final consumption expenditure	3 090.9	3 448.3	3 906.6	4 443.2	5 132.0
Property income payable	290.4	509.3	900.0	1 318.7	1 319.2
Subsidies	575.8	703.6	738.7	652.2	609.6
Social security benefits	3 232.1	3 642.9	4 168.1	4 675.5	5 178.4
Miscellaneous current transfers	355.2	364.1	461.9	631.8	698.3
Statistical discrepancy	9.6	8.8	14.1	57.0	13.4
Gross saving	11.2	−179.5	−392.3	−126.7	634.1
Capital account					
Receipts					
Gross saving	11.2	−179.5	−392.3	−126.7	634.1
Capital transfers	11.2	17.5	59.7	69.1	69.7
Capital taxes	34.2	45.7	58.4	78.6	86.1
Total	56.6	−116.3	−274.2	21.0	789.9
Disbursements					
Gross fixed capital formation	607.7	722.0	994.6	1 029.6	1 238.1
Net purchases of land and intangible assets	24.3	37.9	50.4	53.2	64.3
Capital transfers	491.6	501.8	640.8	768.2	762.6
Net lending (+) or net borrowing (−)	−1 067.1	−1 378.1	−1 960.0	−1 830.0	1 275.1
(Per cent of GDP)	(−4.7)	(−5.3)	(−7.0)	(−5.7)	(−3.6)

1. These accounts are on an ESA basis.
Source: National Institute of Statistics.

102

Table C. **Public sector accounts** *(cont'd)*

Billion pesetas

		1983	1984	1985	1986	1987
		2. Central government				
1.	Tax revenue	2 736.2	3 118.8	3 386.5	4 356.4	5 119.7
2.	Property and entrepreneurial income (gross)	265.2	200.3	266.0	275.2	212.8
3.	Current transfers	684.4	756.8	855.8	954.5	1 066.3
4.	Total current revenue	3 685.8	4 075.9	4 508.3	5 586.1	6 398.8
5.	Purchase of goods and services	1 703.7	1 740.8	1 872.4	2 048.5	2 373.4
6.	Current transfers	1 582.7	1 837.2	2 044.9	2 532.7	2 760.5
7.	Subsidies	484.8	584.6	561.2	436.9	408.4
8.	Others	203.2	410.4	776.1	1 148.4	1 127.8
9.	Total current expenditure	3 974.4	4 573.0	5 254.6	6 166.5	6 670.1
10.	Gross saving	−206.5	−404.2	−643.5	−472.3	−154.3
11.	Capital taxes	23.6	15.5	12.5	7.6	8.0
12.	Capital transfers	2.5	2.7	18.8	104.1	119.7
13.	Total capital resources (10 to 12)	−180.4	−386.0	−612.2	−360.6	−26.6
14.	Gross fixed capital formation	357.3	321.1	342.2	337.3	409.9
15.	Capital transfers	512.3	655.0	745.9	911.5	868.2
16.	Total capital expenditure (14 to 15)	869.6	976.1	1 088.1	1 248.8	1 278.1
17.	Overall financial surplus (+) or deficit (−) (13 *less* 16)	−1 050.0	−1 362.1	−1 700.3	−1 609.4	−1 304.7

Table C. **Public sector accounts** *(cont'd)*

Billion pesetas

	1983	1984	1985	1986	1987
	3. Territorial governments[1]				
1. Tax revenue	918.4	1 241.9	1 688.6	1 928.9	2 552.7
2. Property and entrepreneurial income (gross)	29.0	36.4	45.4	67.5	40.0
3. Current transfers	315.7	397.1	357.4	476.9	385.5
4. Total current revenue	1 263.1	1 675.4	2 091.4	2 473.3	2 978.2
5. Purchase of goods and services	803.4	1 059.6	1 310.6	1 471.5	1 661.0
6. Current transfers	158.8	251.9	260.2	403.1	406.8
7. Others	176.3	216.2	290.2	339.2	385.8
8. Total current expenditure	1 138.5	1 527.7	1 861.0	2 213.8	2 453.6
9. Gross saving	160.2	191.0	284.8	322.1	591.8
10. Capital taxes	10.5	30.1	45.9	71.0	78.1
11. Capital transfers	98.4	247.5	254.4	261.6	263.7
12. Total capital resources (9 to 11)	269.1	468.6	585.1	654.7	933.6
13. Gross fixed capital formation	239.8	399.7	653.2	685.3	822.4
14. Capital transfers	73.0	84.0	113.3	127.4	162.9
15. Total capital expenditure (13 to 14)	312.8	483.7	766.5	812.7	985.3
16. Overall financial surplus (+) or deficit (–) (12 *less* 15)	–43.7	–15.1	–181.4	–158.0	–51.7
	4. Social security institutions				
1. Social security contributions	2 767.9	2 988.0	3 323.7	3 755.3	4 224.2
2. Transfers	770.0	957.9	1 118.4	1 378.8	1 656.0
3. Other current receipts	25.8	34.2	33.9	14.0	26.9
4. Total current receipts	3 563.7	3 980.1	4 476.0	5 148.1	5 907.1
5. Purchase of goods and services	583.9	647.9	723.6	923.2	1 097.6
6. Social security benefits	2 863.1	3 248.6	3 709.8	4 168.4	4 620.4
7. Current subsidies and transfers	68.1	60.2	87.9	46.4	6.8
8. Total current expenditure	3 515.1	3 956.7	4 521.3	5 138.0	5 724.8
9. Gross saving	57.5	33.6	–33.5	23.5	196.6
10. Gross capital formation	34.9	39.3	49.5	60.2	70.1
11. Others	0.5	0.4	0.8	35.2	50.2
12. Total capital expenditure (10 to 11)	35.4	39.7	50.3	95.4	120.3
13. Total income from capital	4.4	4.9	6.0	9.3	5.0
14. Overall financial surplus (+) or deficit (–) (9 *plus* 13 *less* 12)	26.6	–1.2	–78.0	–62.6	81.3

1. Regional and local government.
Source: Bank of Spain, *Informe Anual,* 1987, Madrid 1988.

Table D. **Labour market trends**

	1981	1982	1983	1984	1985	1986	1987[2]
	Thousands						
Civilian labour force[1]	13 045	13 206	13 353	13 437	13 542	13 781	14 298
Civilian employment[1]	11 443	11 294	11 170	10 966	10 870	11 111	11 452
Agriculture	2 135	2 087	2 090	2 016	1 975	1 784	1 728
Industry	3 050	2 884	2 817	2 746	2 653	2 697	2 764
Construction	970	942	898	831	790	849	932
Services	5 287	5 382	5 365	5 374	5 451	5 781	6 028
Employees, total	7 766	7 682	7 539	7 331	7 330	7 675	7 996
Unemployment	1 912	2 218	2 486	2 767	2 969	2 959	2 955
	Per cent						
Participation rate, total	49.6	49.6	49.5	49.1	48.7	48.9	49.4
Men	73.4	72.8	72.0	71.1	70.1	69.7	69.1
Women	28.1	28.7	29.3	29.2	29.3	30.0	31.5
Unemployment rate, total	14.7	16.8	18.6	20.6	21.9	21.5	20.7
Men	13.0	14.6	16.2	17.9	18.8	18.0	16.8
Women	17.5	20.5	22.6	25.0	27.2	27.4	28.0
Less than 25 years old	34.3	38.3	41.8	45.3	46.7	45.1	43.0
25-54 years old	9.3	10.9	12.5	14.1	15.7	15.3	15.0
Over 55 years old	5.7	6.7	7.3	8.9	9.6	10.5	9.4

1. These exclude those who are on compulsory service, but include the professional military as well as marginal workers.
2. Because of a change in the methodology 1987 data are not strictly comparable with earlier years.
Source: Ministry of Labour and Social Security.

Table E. Price and wage trends

Percentage change, annual rate

	1981	1982	1983	1984	1985	1986	1987	1988
	Prices							
Consumer prices	14.6	14.4	12.2	11.3	8.8	8.8	5.2	4.8
Food	13.6	15.0	10.7	12.6	9.5	10.6	5.0	3.7
Non-food	15.1	14.1	13.0	10.6	8.4	7.9	5.4	5.4
Energy	32.4	10.6	16.2	10.5	4.5	−6.2	−3.9	−0.8
Non-energy	13.5	14.7	11.9	11.4	9.1	9.9	5.8	5.1
Non-food and non-energy	13.4	14.5	12.6	10.6	8.9	9.4	6.2	6.0
Industrial prices	15.7	12.4	14.0	12.2	8.0	0.9	0.8	3.0
Food	14.3	14.2	11.2	13.5	6.8	4.2	1.7	1.9
Non-food	9.5	11.4	13.7	10.0	8.1	5.6	5.0	4.0
Investment goods	14.2	12.7	13.1	10.1	8.3	6.2	5.0	4.7
Consumer goods	11.0	12.4	12.9	11.2	7.7	5.1	3.9	3.3
Intermediate goods	19.4	12.4	15.0	13.4	8.0	−3.1	−2.4	2.2
of which: Energy	39.0	12.7	19.0	8.4	8.8	−11.1	−7.0	0.5
Unit value of exports	17.5	13.0	18.5	12.5	7.3	−3.3	3.2	5.3
Unit value of imports	30.6	12.8	20.7	10.1	2.4	−17.3	0.8	2.5
Non-energy	..	13.3	23.2	12.0	2.8	−1.8	0.5	2.9
	Wages							
Average increase in contractual wages	13.0	12.0	11.4	7.8	7.9	8.2	6.5	5.3
Monthly earnings per employee	15.4	14.0	13.7	9.9	9.3	10.9	7.8	7.6
Daily pay in agriculture	11.9	9.3	9.0	8.8	9.2	8.0	7.4	6.2
Salary cost per head in construction (including social security contributions)	15.1	13.4	12.2	10.5	7.4	9.3	7.3	..

Sources: Bank of Spain, *Boletin Estadistico* and Ministry of Finance, *Sintesis Mensual de Indicatores Economicos.*

Table F. Money and credit

Billion pesetas

	1987 Q3	1987 Q4	1988 Q1	1988 Q2	1988 Q3	1988 Q4	1989 Q1
	1. Monetary indicators *(quarterly changes)*						
M1	312.0	413.3	50.8	622.6	561.5	440.7	..
of which:							
Currency in circulation	182.2	−108.2	88.3	184.9	287.9	145.3	..
Sight deposits	130.8	521.5	−37.5	437.7	273.6	295.4	..
Savings deposits	223.9	271.6	−56.0	168.5	276.6	427.1	..
Time deposits	85.7	−192.3	260.0	−20.6	20.7	17.9	..
M3	682.1	374.2	301.8	792.6	890.8	708.0	..
Other liquid assets in the hands of the public	563.8	929.8	368.2	−19.8	12.7	532.5	..
ALP (liquid assets in the hands of the public)	1 245.9	1 304.1	669.9	772.9	903.5	1 240.5	..

107

Table F. **Money and credit** *(cont'd)*

Billion pesetas

	1983	1984	1985	1986	1987	1988
	2. **Monetary indicators** *(end of period, levels)*					
A. ALP (liquid assets in the hands of the public)	20 369	23 083	26 072	29 263	33 252	36 689
a) M1	5 248	5 650	6 327	7 152	8 238	9 708
of which: Currency in circulation	1 686	1 862	2 081	2 402	2 736	3 241
Sight deposits	3 562	3 788	4 246	4 750	5 502	6 467
b) M2	9 731	10 427	11 627	13 127	14 666	16 952
of which: Savings deposits	4 483	4 777	5 300	5 975	6 428	7 244
c) M3	18 739	20 986	22 135	23 001	24 781	27 345
of which: Time deposits	9 007	10 559	10 508	9 874	10 115	10 393
d) Other liquid assets in the hands of the public	1 631	2 098	3 937	6 262	8 472	9 344
B. Non-monetary liabilities	1 644	2 123	2 554	2 832	3 428	4 831
a) General government	961	1 157	1 266	1 269	1 419	1 775
b) Private sector	683	966	1 288	1 563	2 009	3 056
	3. **Credit aggregates** *(end of period, levels)*					
C. Internal credit	22 069	24 635	28 287	31 961	36 355	41 657
a) Credit to general government	4 160	6 401	8 694	10 718	12 183	13 628
of which: Bank credits	2 986	2 369	3 041	2 592	2 446	2 391
Securities	2 509	5 592	6 985	9 169	10 548	10 654
Money market credits	417	464	772	1 047	1 302	1 073
Other	-1 752	-2 024	-2 104	-2 090	-2 113	-490
b) Credit to private sector	17 374	17 644	18 907	20 624	23 601	27 512
of which: Bank credits	15 723	15 912	17 299	19 051	22 045	25 580
Securities	1 493	1 614	1 516	1 591	1 566	1 934
Money market credits	158	118	92	-18	-10	-2
c) Credit to public enterprises	535	590	686	619	571	518
D. Credit to foreign sector	464	1 251	1 417	1 687	2 755	3 057

Source: Bank of Spain.

Table G. **Balance of payments**[1]

Million dollars

	1980	1981	1982	1983	1984	1985	1986[3]	1987[3]
Imports (fob)	32 430	30 953	30 088	27 475	26 954	27 992	33 163	46 122
Exports (fob)	20 688	20 704	20 230	19 974	22 721	23 544	26 713	33 284
Trade Balance	−11 742	−10 249	−9 858	−7 501	−4 233	−4 448	−6 450	−12 837
Services, net	4 885	3 709	3 768	3 885	5 230	5 835	9 262	10 239
of which:								
Tourism	5 752	5 790	6 153	6 003	6 922	7 087	10 442	12 827
Investment income	−1 739	−2 552	−2 549	−2 464	−2 395	−1 808	−1 993	−2 774
Transfers, net	1 557	1 425	1 387	1 163	1 089	1 100	1 128	2 615
Current balance	−5 301	−5 115	−4 704	−2 454	2 086	2 487	3 940	16
Private long-term capital	4 498	4 057	1 738	2 366	2 694	−1 364	572	9 290
Official long-term capital	182	633	992	995	470	−36	−2 117	−170
Banking sector long-term capital	967	276	−405	−121	−306	−1 181	−1 781	−624
Total long-term capital	5 647	4 966	2 325	3 240	2 858	−2 581	−3 326	8 496
Basic balance	346	−149	−2 379	786	4 944	−94	614	8 512
Short-term capital[2]	−254	417	344	341	580	63	579	5 241
Monetary movements (increase in assets=−)	1 725	1 810	3 672	899	−3 076	1 305	−1 245	−12 430
Changes in reserves (increase in reserve=−)	759	757	3 121	301	−4 560	1 304	−2 403	−12 897
Errors and omissions	−1 818	−2 078	−1 637	−2 187	−2 448	−1 274	52	−1 324

1. Transactions basis.
2. Including banks' local accounts in foreign currency.
3. Provisional.
Source: Ministry of Economy and Commerce.

Table H. Foreign trade[1]

1. By commodity
Billion pesetas

	1980	1981	1982	1983	1984	1985	1986	1987
				1. Imports, cif				
1. Live animals and related products	57.60	66.33	84.74	86.19	100.61	117.16	188.86	242.11
2. Vegetables	193.70	223.40	259.51	324.38	308.47	274.39	285.18	248.44
3. Oil and fats	11.15	12.64	11.08	12.63	17.89	19.92	21.77	23.93
4. Food products, beverages and tobacco	52.53	62.29	78.84	120.54	144.18	152.56	168.28	200.04
5. Mineral products	1 006.35	1 333.17	1 455.34	1 764.66	1 852.45	1 951.69	1 037.31	1 084.09
6. Chemicals and related products	175.80	210.36	230.21	283.33	333.37	373.47	463.33	539.86
7. Artificial plastics materials	56.56	64.08	76.99	98.67	119.13	137.21	179.28	220.06
8. Leather, leather manufactures	19.92	26.61	29.33	33.68	57.41	68.32	73.14	98.15
9. Cork and wood products	39.89	30.23	31.54	41.53	45.25	55.93	62.39	77.13
10. Ruper, articles of paper pulp	42.47	48.55	63.54	65.72	84.73	96.74	125.26	153.89
11. Textile and related products	62.12	64.26	78.47	101.00	111.14	129.42	164.21	216.00
12. Footwear, hat-making	4.42	4.14	5.38	6.58	6.45	8.50	12.34	17.74
13. Mineral manufactures, plaster, glass	23.17	23.73	27.37	32.23	34.81	40.11	52.37	68.93
14. Pearls, precious stones, jewellery	28.33	24.70	42.99	58.39	50.74	49.41	25.85	26.51
15. Manufactures of metal	157.99	166.04	213.82	223.99	274.15	344.16	391.51	402.55
16. Machinery and electrical machinery	307.35	360.15	462.82	545.58	658.81	775.11	979.22	1 329.51
17. Transport equipment	113.74	134.42	163.86	179.42	226.00	275.44	413.99	685.85
18. Optical instruments, photographic apparatus, sound equipment	76.95	99.85	133.99	171.79	174.47	200.77	261.60	307.53
19. Arms and ammunition	2.49	1.99	2.02	1.49	0.99	1.40	2.18	1.88
20. Furniture, toys, sporting goods	16.68	17.27	21.04	23.31	23.68	27.72	39.85	61.52
21. Works of art, antiques	1.46	1.77	1.92	1.92	2.23	10.54	6.64	24.10
00. Not classified	–	–	–	–	3.16	4.75	0.53	–

1. Live animals and related products	22.67	35.36	31.82	41.36	48.69	55.05	58.42	70.88
2. Vegetables	131.55	180.43	179.82	209.65	273.36	285.86	350.25	418.58
3. Oils and fats	33.99	30.87	31.51	45.73	70.56	80.52	47.23	64.07
4. Food products, beverages and tobacco	87.52	110.69	126.19	162.29	205.21	206.40	189.69	218.13
5. Mineral products	104.56	164.01	238.77	344.94	429.65	457.56	300.69	319.89
6. Chemicals and related products	94.51	119.60	138.05	181.28	241.71	282.54	253.33	297.97
7. Artificial plastics materials	58.88	66.60	78.02	101.34	138.46	158.12	154.71	186.29
8. Leather, leather manufactures	29.99	34.66	35.33	40.92	55.16	66.41	73.63	88.13
9. Cork and wood products	23.13	25.99	30.78	40.47	48.82	48.98	43.36	43.98
10. Ruper, articles of paper pulp	59.68	72.35	85.24	95.26	114.40	123.32	126.00	145.08
11. Textile and related products	73.35	96.38	102.32	135.71	182.75	195.00	178.30	196.23
12. Footwear, hat-making	43.28	58.81	67.32	91.74	128.67	145.44	138.29	140.59
13. Mineral manufactures, plaster, glass	38.98	52.91	56.02	77.87	96.66	96.32	100.43	114.55
14. Pearls, precious stones, jewellery	20.15	23.67	21.41	49.41	49.66	36.10	27.73	27.11
15. Manufactures of metal	243.40	295.41	343.95	419.34	550.61	630.44	468.64	419.70
16. Machinery and electrical machinery	192.04	244.90	287.29	295.57	405.91	485.16	505.85	564.76
17. Transport equipment	198.38	231.01	320.72	445.95	596.17	628.09	664.51	738.58
18. Optical instruments, photographic apparatus, sound equipment	11.66	14.46	16.72	19.71	21.00	29.59	34.18	37.93
19. Arms and ammunition	3.51	3.15	6.95	4.48	5.87	6.29	5.07	6.15
20. Furniture, toys, sporting goods	21.20	27.51	33.47	42.18	56.36	61.32	68.00	80.15
21. Works of art, antiques	0.77	0.97	2.23	1.51	1.06	6.81	17.02	16.88
00. Not classified	–	–	–	–	22.71	23.41	9.47	–
Total	1 493.20	1 889.72	2 233.94	2 846.71	3 720.74	4 085.32	3 805.33	4 195.63

1. Customs basis.
Source: Ministry of Economy and Commerce.

Table H. **Foreign trade**[1] *(cont'd)*

2. By geographical area

Billion pesetas

	1980	1981	1982	1983	1984	1985	1986	1987
	1. Imports, cif							
Total	2 477.1	2 970.4	3 465.5	4 176.5	4 629.0	5 073.2	4 890.8	6 029.8
OECD	1 294.3	1 518.1	1 883.8	2 241.9	2 499.0	2 883.2	3 500.2	4 458.0
of which:								
United States	323.7	412.4	478.3	495.5	519.3	553.0	482.7	499.1
Japan	62.5	79.4	110.5	139.9	141.8	172.8	240.1	270.2
Canada	19.6	20.6	20.8	23.6	22.2	21.3	19.2	26.4
EEC, total	777.3	874.3	1 100.5	1 373.5	1 583.6	1 868.5	2 458.1	3 292.0
of which:								
United Kingdom	117.0	132.9	170.4	256.7	281.1	329.6	377.7	421.8
France	205.3	237.6	275.3	344.3	398.0	471.1	571.4	774.0
Germany	203.3	241.5	328.2	366.1	458.7	537.4	736.1	970.3
Italy	122.0	118.4	155.5	180.9	195.3	232.7	356.9	532.7
Portugal	11.8	12.5	16.5	24.6	36.1	40.1	63.1	100.7
Non OECD countries	1 182.8	1 452.3	1 581.7	1 934.6	2 130.0	2 190.0	1 390.6	1 571.8
of which:								
COMECON	55.8	78.0	94.5	124.1	144.1	119.3	86.2	155.8
OPEC	685.8	901.3	926.7	1 038.0	1 118.7	1 021.6	551.1	572.6
Latin America	210.6	293.1	329.3	476.4	514.5	538.9	334.1	362.4
Other	230.6	179.9	231.2	296.1	352.7	510.2	419.2	481.0
	2. Exports, fob							
Total	1 524.1	1 888.4	2 258.0	2 837.5	3 775.5	4 101.7	3 798.4	4 193.4
OECD	981.0	1 126.9	1 390.6	1 842.8	2 614.8	2 879.6	2 936.5	3 334.9
of which:								
United States	81.1	126.9	145.5	206.6	360.3	407.7	348.8	341.2
Japan	20.8	30.0	28.3	43.5	58.9	53.5	42.5	46.3
Canada	10.7	16.6	15.1	20.6	36.8	42.1	43.0	44.3
EEC, total	795.2	868.2	1098.1	1 424.8	1 943.5	2 146.3	2 292.1	2 676.6
of which:								
United Kingdom	107.3	130.6	160.7	219.9	343.0	351.3	335.3	398.0
France	253.4	270.6	369.9	448.7	566.6	636.4	682.7	786.8
Germany	155.7	163.3	185.1	260.2	361.8	393.1	444.6	503.3
Italy	117.4	108.0	127.1	150.8	225.6	289.5	302.3	371.8
Portugal	41.4	558.0	62.8	54.3	90.3	91.2	130.9	189.8
Non OECD countries	543.1	761.5	867.4	994.7	1 160.7	1 222.1	861.9	858.5
of which:								
COMECON	41.3	73.0	48.2	74.1	93.8	120.9	68.5	66.9
OPEC	196.0	278.6	337.7	394.7	342.0	295.8	212.2	192.1
Latin America	130.0	163.4	182.5	154.3	176.5	208.1	180.0	147.6
Other	175.8	246.5	299.0	371.6	548.4	597.3	401.2	451.9

1. Customs basis.
Source: Ministry of Economy and Commerce.

Table I.   **Foreign assets and liabilities**

Billion pesetas, end of period

	1983	1984	1985	1986	1987
Liabilities	8 204.7	9 682.8	9 117.5	9 051.8	10 210.3
Monetary institutions	3 435.0	4 080.5	3 620.3	3 798.2	4 134.4
Bank of Spain	35.3	42.9	46.8	47.7	45.8
Banking system	3 399.7	4 037.6	3 573.5	3 750.5	4 088.6
Government	587.8	768.8	737.0	493.8	542.5
Private sector	4 181.9	4 833.5	4 760.2	4 760.0	5 533.4
Foreign investments	754.1	940.6	1 185.8	1 698.8	2 371.8
Assets	4 406.1	6 011.1	5 748.9	6 034.7	7 271.8
Monetary institutions	3 805.4	5 229.7	4 901.3	5 205.9	6 541.6
Bank of Spain	1 234.9	2 089.9	1 702.9	1 932.6	3 597.4
Banking system	2 570.5	3 139.8	3 198.4	3 273.3	2 944.2
Government	20.4	35.3	38.4	68.4	97.7
Private sector	580.3	746.1	809.0	760.7	632.5
Investment abroad	512.9	603.4	610.2	603.9	604.6

Source: Bank of Spain.

STATISTICAL ANNEX

BASIC STATISTICS :
INTERNATIONAL COMPARISONS

	Units	Reference period[1]	Australia	Austria
Population				
Total	Thousands	1987	16 249	7 575
Inhabitants per sq.km	Number		2	90
Net average annual increase over previous 10 years	%		1.4	0.0
Employment				
Total civilian employment (TCE)[2]	Thousands	1987	7 079	32 997
of which: Agriculture	% of TCE		5.8	8.6
Industry	% of TCE		26.6	37.7
Services	% of TCE		67.6	53.7
Gross domestic product (GDP)				
At current prices and current exchange rates	Billion US$	1987	193.7	117.2
Per capita	US$		11 919	15 470
At current prices using current PPP's[3]	Billion US$	1987	204.9	88.4
Per capita	US$		12 612	11 664
Average annual volume growth over previous 5 years . . .	%	1987	3.7	1.8
Gross fixed capital formation (GFCF)	% of GDP	1987	23.8	22.6
of which: Machinery and equipment	% of GDP		11.5 (86)	9.7
Residential construction	% of GDP		4.7 (86)	4.6 (86
Average annual volume growth over previous 5 years . . .	%	1987	1.7	2.3
Gross saving ratio[4]	% of GDP	1987	20.3	24.1
General government				
Current expenditure on goods and services	% of GDP	1987	18.2	19.0
Current disbursements[5]	% of GDP	1987	35.0 (86)	46.6 (86
Current receipts	% of GDP	1987	34.7 (86)	47.9 (86
Net official development assistance	% of GNP	1987	0.33	0.17
Indicators of living standards				
Private consumption per capita using current PPP's[3] . . .	US$	1987	7 389	6 535
Passenger cars, per 1 000 inhabitants	Number	1985	. .	306 (81
Telephones, per 1 000 inhabitants	Number	1985	540 (83)	460 (83
Television sets, per 1 000 inhabitants	Number	1985	. .	300 (81
Doctors, per 1 000 inhabitants	Number	1985	. .	1.7 (82
Infant mortality per 1 000 live births	Number	1985	9.2 (84)	11.0
Wages and prices (average annual increase over previous 5 years)				
Wages (earnings or rates according to availability)	%	1987	5.7	4.9
Consumer prices	%	1987	7.0	3.0
Foreign trade				
Exports of goods, fob*	Million US$	1987	26 484	27 084
as % of GDP	%		13.6	23.0
average annual increase over previous 5 years	%		4.4	11.6
Imports of goods, cif*	Million US$	1987	26 964	32 580
as % of GDP	%		13.9	27.7
average annual increase over previous 5 years	%		2.8	10.8
Total official reserves[6]	Million SDR's	1987	6 441	6 049
As ratio of average monthly imports of goods	Ratio		3.4	2.6

* At current prices and exchange rates.
1. Unless otherwise stated.
2. According to the definitions used in OECD *Labour force Statistics*.
3. PPP's = Purchasing Power Parities.
4. Gross saving = Gross national disposable income *minus* Private and Government consumption.
5. Current disbursements = Current expenditure on goods and services *plus* current transfers and payments of property income.
6. Gold included in reserves is valued at 35 SDR's per ounce. End of year.
7. Including Luxembourg.
8. Included in Belgium.
9. Including non-residential construction.

Belgium	Canada	Denmark	Finland	France	Germany	Greece	Iceland	Ireland	Italy	Japan	Luxembourg	Netherlands	New Zealand	Norway	Portugal	Spain	Sweden	Switzerland	Turkey	United Kingdom	United States	Yugoslavia
9 868	25 803	5 130	4 932	55 627	61 149	9 998	245	3 542	57 331	122 091	372	14 671	3 284	4 184	10 280	38 830	8 399	6 610	52 010	56 890	243 915	23 410
324	3	119	15	102	246	76	2	50	190	328	143	432	12	13	112	77	19	160	67	232	26	90
0.0	1.0	0.1	0.4	0.4	0.0	0.7	1.0	0.8	0.3	0.7	0.3	0.6	0.5	0.3	0.5	0.7	0.2	0.5	2.2	0.1	1.0	0.8
3 645 (86)	11 954	2 630 (86)	2 414	20 988	25 456	3 601 (86)	117 (86)	1 068 (86)	20 584	59 110	164 (86)	5 135 (86)	1 517 (86)	2 090	4 156	11 370	4 337	3 219 (86)	15 632 (86)	24 987	112 440	..
2.9	4.9	5.9	10.4	7.1	5.2	28.5	10.3	15.7	10.5	8.3	3.7	4.9	10.5	6.7	21.9	16.1	4.2	6.5	55.7	2.4	3.0	..
29.7	25.3	28.2	31.2	30.8	40.5	28.1	36.8	28.7	32.6	33.8	32.9	25.5	28.9	27.0	35.8	32.0	30.2	37.7	18.1	29.8	27.1	..
67.4	69.8	65.9	58.4	62.1	54.3	43.4	53.0	55.5	56.8	57.9	63.4	69.6	60.6	66.3	42.3	51.8	65.6	55.8	26.2	67.8	69.9	..
138.9	410.9	101.3	89.5	879.9	1 117.8	47.2	5.3	29.4	758.1	2 376.5	6.0	213.2	35.1	82.7	36.7	289.2	158.5	171.1	67.4	669.8	4 472.9	61.7 (86)
14 071	16 019	19 750	18 151	15 818	18 280	4 719	21 813	8 297	13 224	19 465	16 138	14 530	10 620	19 756	3 761	7 449	18 876	25 848	1 296	11 765	18 338	2 652 (86)
116.5	444.5	68.4	63.3	712.2	814.7	63.6	3.8	26.7	702.5	1 609.4	5.5	179.7	35.3	64.5	61.4	337.1	115.7	104.9	220.9	702.5	4 472.9	..
11 802	17 211	13 329	12 838	12 803	13 323	6 363	15 508	7 541	12 254	13 182	14 705	12 252	10 680	15 405	6 297	8 681	13 771	15 842	4 247	12 340	18 338	..
1.5	4.2	2.7	3.2	1.6	2.1	1.4	3.1	1.8	2.6	3.9	4.0	2.1	2.1	4.1	2.1	2.9	2.4	2.3	6.0	3.2	4.3	..
16.3	21.0	18.8	23.5	19.4	19.4	17.4	18.8	17.4	19.9	28.9	22.6	20.3	21.2	28.0	25.3	20.7	19.0	25.2	24.5	17.3	17.3	21.6 (86)
7.0 (86)	6.9 (86)	7.8	9.7	8.3	8.4	7.1	6.5	9.4 (86)	10.0	10.5 (86)	9.0 (82)	10.0	13.1 (85)	7.9 (86)	14.7 (81)	6.4 (86)	8.5 (86)	8.8	8.6 (84)	8.1 (86)	7.6	..
3.4	6.4 (86)	4.4	55	5.2	5.2	4.6	3.5	4.6 (86)	5.2	5.0 (86)	4.7 (82)	5.2	4.6 (85)	5.0 (86)	6.4 (81)	4.0 (86)	3.8 (86)	16.4 (9)	2.7 (84)	3.8 (86)	5.0	..
2.0	4.8	6.5	1.9	0.6	1.8	-2.2	1.8	-3.7	2.8	5.3	0.8	4.8	2.0	4.1	-0.7	3.8	3.6	6.0	7.3	4.7	7.0	..
17.6	18.8	15.5	22.5	19.6	23.9	14.7	15.2	18.6	20.9	32.3	56.5	21.8	20.3	23.4	27.5	21.9	18.0	31.7	24.1	17.2	14.7	..
16.3	19.5	25.4	20.7	19.1	19.8	19.5	17.7	18.0	16.7	9.6	16.7	16.1	17.6	20.9	14.4	14.4	26.7	12.8	9.1	20.9	18.6	14.3 (86)
51.6 (86)	43.3 (86)	53.4 (86)	38.2	48.4	43.0 (86)	42.9 (86)	27.3 (86)	49.2 (84)	45.2	39.3 (86)	45.3 (84)	54.0 (86)	..	47.8 (86)	37.6 (81)	36.1 (86)	60.0 (86)	30.1	..	42.9 (86)	35.5 (86)	..
45.0 (86)	39.4 (86)	58.0 (86)	39.6	49.4	44.9 (86)	36.6 (86)	32.1 (86)	43.3 (84)	39.3 (86)	31.3 (86)	54.1 (84)	52.8 (86)	..	56.5 (86)	33.3 (81)	35.0 (86)	61.6 (86)	34.5	..	41.6 (86)	31.2 (86)	..
0.49	0.47	0.88	0.50	0.74	0.39	..	0.05	0.20	0.35	0.31	0.10	0.98	0.26	1.09	0.08	0.06	0.88	0.31	..	0.28	0.20	..
7 593	10 059	7 236	6 966	7 796	7 374	4 273	9 930*	4 378	7 543	7 623	8 694	7 461	6 236	8 155	4 167	5 521	7 273	9 349*	2 844	7 731	12 232	1 335 (86)*
335 (84)	421 (82)	293	329 (86)	369 (86)	441 (86)	127	431	206 (83)	355 (84)	221 (83)	439 (87)	341	455	382 (86)	135 (82)	252	377	402	18 (82)	312 (83)	473 (84)	121 (83)
414 (83)	664 (83)	783	615	614 (86)	641 (86)	373	525 (83)	235 (83)	448 (84)	535 (83)	425 (86)	410 (86)	646	622 (84)	166 (83)	381 (86)	890 (83)	1 334	55 (83)	521 (84)	650 (84)	122 (83)
303 (84)	471 (80)	392	370 (86)	394 (86)	377 (86)	158 (80)	303	181 (80)	244 (84)	250 (80)	336 (83)	317 (86)	291	346 (86)	140 (80)	256 (82)	390	337	76 (79)	336 (84)	621 (80)	175 (83)
2.8 (84)	1.8 (82)	2.5 (84)	2.3 (86)	2.3 (86)	2.5 (84)	2.8 (83)	2.4 (84)	1.3 (82)	3.6 (82)	1.3 (82)	1.9 (86)	2.2 (84)	2.4	2.2	1.8 (82)	3.4 (86)	2.5	1.4 (84)	1.5 (83)	0.5 (83)	2.0 (85)	1.6 (82)
9.4	9.1 (83)	7.9	5.8 (86)	7.0 (86)	9.1	14.1	5.7	8.9	10.9	5.9 (84)	9.0	9.6 (86)	10.8	8.5 (86)	17.8	7.0 (84)	6.8	6.9	..	9.4	10.4 (86)	31.7 (83)
3.4	3.6	6.1	8.5	6.4	3.6	17.4	..	8.8	10.5	2.6	..	2.3	7.4	10.2	17.9	10.3	7.6	..	..	8.5	3.1	..
3.5	4.2	4.7	5.0	4.7	1.1	19.3	25.7	5.2	7.6	1.1	2.2	1.3	12.6	7.0	17.2	8.5	5.9	2.1	41.6	4.7	3.3	56.3
82 824[7]	94 320	25 632	19 404	147 936	293 424	6 516	1 368	15 948	116 004	230 220	..[8]	92 592	7 164	21 804	9 144	33 972	44 388	45 312	10 344	130 632	254 124	11 425
59.8	22.8	25.3	22.1	16.8	26.2	13.9	25.8	54.8	15.4	9.7	..	43.1	20.1	26.2	25.3	11.8	27.9	26.6	15.7	19.7	5.7	16.3
9.6	6.5	11.1	8.2	9.0	10.7	8.7	13.7	14.6	9.6	12.1	..	6.9	3.4	4.4	17.0	10.4	10.6	11.8	12.1	7.7	3.7	2.2
82 992[7]	87 528	25 452	18 828	153 204	227 916	13 116	1 584	13 620	124 596	150 300	..	91 068	7 224	22 428	13 248	48 816	40 596	50 424	14 460	153 768	424 440	12 603
59.9	21.1	25.1	21.4	17.4	20.4	27.9	29.9	46.8	16.6	6.3	..	42.4	20.2	27.0	36.7	17.0	25.5	29.6	21.9	17.0	9.6	18.5
7.4	9.7	8.8	7.0	6.7	6.5	5.6	10.8	5.9	7.7	2.8	..	7.2	4.6	7.8	6.9	9.1	8.0	12.0	9.7	9.1	11.7	-3.1
7 958[7]	5 778	7 153	4 592	26 161	58 846	2 007	221	3 393	23 631	57 925	..	12 818	2 298	10 105	3 047	22 035	5 974	22 283	1 254	30 070	33 657	557
1.4	0.9	4.0	3.5	2.4	3.7	2.2	2.0	3.5	2.7	5.5	..	2.0	4.5	6.4	3.3	6.4	2.1	6.3	1.2	2.8	1.1	0.6

Sources:
Population and Employment: OECD Labour Force Statistics.
GDP, GFCF, and General Government: OECD National Accounts. Vol. I and OECD Economic Outlook,
Historical Statistics.
Indicators of living standards: Miscellaneous national publications.
Wages and Prices: OECD Main Economic Indicators.
Foreign trade: OECD Monthly Foreign trade Statistics, series A.
Total official reserves: IMF International Financial Statistics.

EMPLOYMENT OPPORTUNITIES

Economics and Statistics Department, OECD

The Economics and Statistics Department of the OECD offers challenging and rewarding opportunities to economists interested in applied policy analysis in an international environment. The Department's concerns extend across the entire field of economic policy analysis, both macroeconomic and microeconomic, and it is also responsible for the collection, processing and dissemination of a wide range of internationally consistent statistics. On the economic side, its main task is to provide, for discussion by committees of senior officials from Member countries, documents and papers dealing with current policy concerns. Within this programme of work, three major responsibilities are :

– To prepare regular surveys of the economies of individual Member countries;
– To issue full twice-yearly reviews of the economic situation and prospects of the OECD countries in the context of world economic trends;
– To analyse specific policy issues in a medium-term context for the OECD as a whole, and to a lesser extent for the non-OECD countries.

The documents prepared for these purposes, together with much of the Department's other economic work and its statistical output, appear in published form in *OECD Economic Outlook*, *OECD Economic Surveys*, *OECD Economic Studies*, the Department's Working Paper series, and an extensive list of statistical publications.

The Department maintains a world econometric model, INTERLINK, which plays an important role in the preparation of the policy analyses and twice-yearly projections. The availability of extensive cross-country databases and good computer resources facilitates comparative empirical analysis, much of which is incorporated into the model.

The Department is made up of about 90 professional economists and statisticians from a variety of backgrounds from all Member countries. Most projects are done by small teams and last from four to eighteen months. Within the Department, ideas and points of view are widely discussed; there is a lively professional interchange; and all professional staff have the opportunity to contribute actively to the programme of work.

Skills ESD is looking for

a) Solid competence in using the tools of both microeconomic and macroeconomic theory to answer policy questions. In our experience, this requires the equivalent of a PhD in economics or substantial relevant professional experience to compensate for a lower degree.

b) Solid knowledge of economic statistics and quantitative methods; this includes how to identify data, estimate structural relationships, apply and interpret basic techniques of time series analysis, and test hypotheses. It is essential to be able to interpret results sensibly in an economic policy context.

c) A keen interest in and knowledge of policy issues, economic developments and their political/social contexts.

d) Interest and experience in analysing questions posed by policy-makers and presenting the results to them effectively and judiciously. Thus work experience in government agencies or policy research institutions is an advantage.

e) The ability to write clearly, effectively and to the point. The OECD is a bilingual organisation with French and English as the official languages. Candidates must have excellent knowledge of one of these languages and some knowledge of the other. Knowledge of other languages might also be an advantage for certain posts.

f) For some posts, expertise in a particular area may be important, but a successful candidate can expect to be asked to contribute in a broader range of topics relevant to the work of the Department. Thus, except in rare cases, the Department does not recruit narrow specialists.

g) The Department works on a tight time schedule and strict deadlines. Moreover, much of the work in the Department is carried out in small groups of economists. Thus, the ability to work with other economists, from a variety of professional backgrounds, and to produce work on time is important.

General Information

The salary for recruits depends on educational and professional back-ground, but positions carry a basic salary from FF 223 584 or FF 275 880 for Administrators (economists) and from FF 320 820 for Principal Administrators (senior economists). This may be supplemented by expatriation and/or family allowances depending on nationality, residence and family situation. Initial appointments are for a fixed term of two to three years.

Vacancies are open to candidates from OECD Member countries. The Organisation seeks to maintain an appropriate balance between female and male staff and among nationals from Member countries.

For further information on employment opportunities in the Economics and Statistics Department, contact :

Executive Assistant
Economics and Statistics Department
OECD
2, rue André-Pascal
75775 PARIS CEDEX 16
France

Applications citing "ECOU", together with a detailed curriculum vitæ in English or French, should be sent to:

Head of Personnel
OECD
2, rue André-Pascal
75775 PARIS CEDEX 16
France

WHERE TO OBTAIN OECD PUBLICATIONS
OÙ OBTENIR LES PUBLICATIONS DE L'OCDE

ARGENTINA - ARGENTINE
Carlos Hirsch S.R.L.,
Florida 165, 4º Piso,
(Galeria Guemes) 1333 Buenos Aires
Tel. 33.1787.2391 y 30.7122

AUSTRALIA - AUSTRALIE
D.A. Book (Aust.) Pty. Ltd.
11-13 Station Street (P.O. Box 163)
Mitcham, Vic. 3132   Tel. (03) 873 4411

AUSTRIA - AUTRICHE
OECD Publications and Information Centre,
4 Simrockstrasse,
5300 Bonn (Germany)   Tel. (0228) 21.60.45
Gerold & Co., Graben 31, Wien 1 Tel. 52.22.35

BELGIUM - BELGIQUE
Jean de Lannoy,
Avenue du Roi 202
B-1060 Bruxelles   Tel. (02) 538.51.69

CANADA
Renouf Publishing Company Ltd
1294 Algoma Road, Ottawa, Ont. K1B 3W8
                          Tel: (613) 741-4333
Stores:
61 rue Sparks St., Ottawa, Ont. K1P 5R1
                          Tel: (613) 238-8985
211 rue Yonge St., Toronto, Ont. M5B 1M4
                          Tel: (416) 363-3171
Federal Publications Inc.,
301-303 King St. W.,
Toronto, Ont. M5V 1J5   Tel. (416)581-1552
Les Éditions la Liberté inc.,
3020 Chemin Sainte-Foy,
Sainte-Foy, P.Q. G1X 3V6, Tel. (418)658-3763

DENMARK - DANEMARK
Munksgaard Export and Subscription Service
35, Nørre Søgade, DK-1370 København K
                          Tel. +45.1.12.85.70

FINLAND - FINLANDE
Akateeminen Kirjakauppa,
Keskuskatu 1, 00100 Helsinki 10 Tel. 0.12141

FRANCE
OCDE/OECD
Mail Orders/Commandes par correspondance :
2, rue André-Pascal,
75775 Paris Cedex 16   Tel. (1) 45.24.82.00
Bookshop/Librairie : 33, rue Octave-Feuillet
75016 Paris
             Tel. (1) 45.24.81.67 et/ou (1) 45.24.81.81
Librairie de l'Université,
12a, rue Nazareth,
13602 Aix-en-Provence   Tel. 42.26.18.08

GERMANY - ALLEMAGNE
OECD Publications and Information Centre,
4 Simrockstrasse,
5300 Bonn   Tel. (0228) 21.60.45

GREECE - GRÈCE
Librairie Kauffmann,
28, rue du Stade, 105 64 Athens Tel. 322.21.60

HONG KONG
Government Information Services,
Publications (Sales) Office,
Information Services Department
No. 1, Battery Path, Central

ICELAND - ISLANDE
Snæbjörn Jónsson & Co., h.f.,
Hafnarstræti 4 & 9,
P.O.B. 1131 - Reykjavik
                          Tel. 13133/14281/11936

INDIA - INDE
Oxford Book and Stationery Co.,
Scindia House, New Delhi 110001
                          Tel. 331.5896/5308
17 Park St., Calcutta 700016   Tel. 240832

INDONESIA - INDONÉSIE
Pdii-Lipi, P.O. Box 3065/JKT.Jakarta
                          Tel. 583467

IRELAND - IRLANDE
TDC Publishers - Library Suppliers,
12 North Frederick Street, Dublin 1
                          Tel. 744835-749677

ITALY - ITALIE
Libreria Commissionaria Sansoni,
Via Benedetto Fortini 120/10,
Casella Post. 552
50125 Firenze   Tel. 055/645415
Via Bartolini 29, 20155 Milano   Tel. 365083
La diffusione delle pubblicazioni OCSE viene
assicurata dalle principali librerie ed anche da :
Editrice e Libreria Herder,
Piazza Montecitorio 120, 00186 Roma
                          Tel. 6794628
Libreria Hœpli,
Via Hœpli 5, 20121 Milano Tel. 865446
Libreria Scientifica
Dott. Lucio de Biasio "Aeiou"
Via Meravigli 16, 20123 Milano   Tel. 807679

JAPAN - JAPON
OECD Publications and Information Centre,
Landic Akasaka Bldg., 2-3-4 Akasaka,
Minato-ku, Tokyo 107   Tel. 586.2016

KOREA - CORÉE
Kyobo Book Centre Co. Ltd.
P.O.Box: Kwang Hwa Moon 1658,
Seoul   Tel. (REP) 730.78.91

LEBANON - LIBAN
Documenta Scientifica/Redico,
Edison Building, Bliss St.,
P.O.B. 5641, Beirut   Tel. 354429-344425

MALAYSIA/SINGAPORE -
MALAISIE/SINGAPOUR
University of Malaya Co-operative Bookshop
Ltd.,
7 Lrg 51A/227A, Petaling Jaya
Malaysia   Tel. 7565000/7565425
Information Publications Pte Ltd
Pei-Fu Industrial Building,
24 New Industrial Road No. 02-06
Singapore 1953   Tel. 2831786, 2831798

NETHERLANDS - PAYS-BAS
SDU Uitgeverij
Christoffel Plantijnstraat 2
Postbus 20014
2500 EA's-Gravenhage   Tel. 070-789911
Voor bestellingen: Tel. 070-789880

NEW ZEALAND - NOUVELLE-ZÉLANDE
Government Printing Office Bookshops:
Auckland: Retail Bookshop, 25 Rutland Stseet,
Mail Orders, 85 Beach Road
Private Bag C.P.O.
Hamilton: Retail: Ward Street,
Mail Orders, P.O. Box 857
Wellington: Retail, Mulgrave Street, (Head
Office)
Cubacade World Trade Centre,
Mail Orders, Private Bag
Christchurch: Retail, 159 Hereford Street,
Mail Orders, Private Bag
Dunedin: Retail, Princes Street,
Mail Orders, P.O. Box 1104

NORWAY - NORVÈGE
Narvesen Info Center - NIC,
Bertrand Narvesens vei 2,
P.O.B. 6125 Etterstad, 0602 Oslo 6
                 Tel. (02) 67.83.10, (02) 68.40.20

PAKISTAN
Mirza Book Agency
65 Shahrah Quaid-E-Azam, Lahore 3 Tel. 66839

PHILIPPINES
I.J. Sagun Enterprises, Inc.
P.O. Box 4322 CPO Manila
                    Tel. 695-1946, 922-9495

PORTUGAL
Livraria Portugal, Rua do Carmo 70-74,
1117 Lisboa Codex   Tel. 360582/3

SINGAPORE/MALAYSIA -
SINGAPOUR/MALAISIE
See "Malaysia/Singapor". Voir
«Malaisie/Singapour»

SPAIN - ESPAGNE
Mundi-Prensa Libros, S.A.,
Castelló 37, Apartado 1223, Madrid-28001
                          Tel. 431.33.99
Libreria Bosch, Ronda Universidad 11,
Barcelona 7   Tel. 317.53.08/317.53.58

SWEDEN - SUÈDE
AB CE Fritzes Kungl. Hovbokhandel,
Box 16356, S 103 27 STH,
Regeringsgatan 12,
DS Stockholm   Tel. (08) 23.89.00
Subscription Agency/Abonnements:
Wennergren-Williams AB,
Box 30004, S104 25 Stockholm Tel. (08)54.12.00

SWITZERLAND - SUISSE
OECD Publications and Information Centre,
4 Simrockstrasse,
5300 Bonn (Germany)   Tel. (0228) 21.60.45
Librairie Payot,
6 rue Grenus, 1211 Genève 11
                          Tel. (022) 31.89.50
Maditec S.A.
Ch. des Palettes 4
1020 - Renens/Lausanne   Tel. (021) 635.08.65
United Nations Bookshop/Librairie des Nations-
Unies
Palais des Nations, 1211 - Geneva 10
                     Tel. 022-34-60-11 (ext. 48 72)

TAIWAN - FORMOSE
Good Faith Worldwide Int'l Co., Ltd.
9th floor, No. 118, Sec.2, Chung Hsiao E. Road
Taipei   Tel. 391.7396/391.7397

THAILAND - THAILANDE
Suksit Siam Co., Ltd., 1715 Rama IV Rd.,
Samyam Bangkok 5   Tel. 2511630
INDEX Book Promotion & Service Ltd.
59/6 Soi Lang Suan, Ploenchit Road
Patjumawwan, Bangkok 10500
                    Tel. 250-1919, 252-1066

TURKEY - TURQUIE
Kültur Yayinlari Is-Türk Ltd. Sti.
Atatürk Bulvari No: 191/Kat. 21
Kavaklidere/Ankara   Tel. 25.07.60
Dolmabahce Cad. No: 29
Besiktas/Istanbul   Tel. 160.71.88

UNITED KINGDOM - ROYAUME-UNI
H.M. Stationery Office,
Postal orders only: (01)873-8483
P.O.B. 276, London SW8 5DT
Telephone orders: (01) 873-9090, or
Personal callers:
49 High Holborn, London WC1V 6HB
Branches at: Belfast, Birmingham,
Bristol, Edinburgh, Manchester

UNITED STATES - ÉTATS-UNIS
OECD Publications and Information Centre,
2001 L Street, N.W., Suite 700,
Washington, D.C. 20036 - 4095
                          Tel. (202) 785.6323

VENEZUELA
Libreria del Este,
Avda F. Miranda 52, Aptdo. 60337,
Edificio Galipan, Caracas 106
             Tel. 951.17.05/951.23.07/951.12.97

YUGOSLAVIA - YOUGOSLAVIE
Jugoslovenska Knjiga, Knez Mihajlova 2,
P.O.B. 36, Beograd   Tel. 621.992

Orders and inquiries from countries where
Distributors have not yet been appointed should be
sent to:
OECD, Publications Service, 2, rue André-Pascal,
75775 PARIS CEDEX 16.

Les commandes provenant de pays où l'OCDE n'a
pas encore désigné de distributeur doivent être
adressées à :
OCDE, Service des Publications. 2, rue André-
Pascal, 75775 PARIS CEDEX 16.

72380-1-1989

OECD PUBLICATIONS
2, rue André-Pascal
75775 PARIS CEDEX 16
No. 44771
(10 89 24 1) ISBN 92-64-13247-3
ISSN 0376-6438

•

PRINTED IN FRANCE